The Twelve
Circus Rings

The Twelve Circus Rings

Seymour Chwast

Gulliver Books

Harcourt Brace Jovanovich, Publishers

SAN DIEGO   NEW YORK   LONDON

For my mother, Esther Newman,
who took me to see Gargantua
— S.C.

HBJ

Copyright © 1993 by Seymour Chwast

Library of Congress Cataloging-in-Publication Data
Chwast, Seymour.
The twelve circus rings/by Seymour Chwast. — 1st ed.
p.   cm.
"Gulliver books."
Summary: Introduces the numbers from one to twelve
using the animals, acrobats, and clowns at the circus.
ISBN 0-15-200627-3
1. Counting — Juvenile literature.   2. Circus — Juvenile literature.
[1. Circus.   2. Counting.]   I. Title.
QA113.C48   1993
513.2'11 — dc20   92-13576
[6]

First edition
A B C D E

The illustrations in this book were done with
a Pilot marker and Cello-tak film.
The text type and display type were set in
ITC Cheltenham Light Condensed by Thompson
Type, San Diego, California.
Color separations by Bright Arts, Ltd., Singapore
Printed and bound by Tien Wah Press, Singapore
Production supervision by Warren Wallerstein
and Fran Wager
Designed by Seymour Chwast and Michael Farmer

Printed in Singapore

In the first circus ring, my sister saw with me a daredevil on a high wire.

In the third circus ring, my sister saw with me three monkeys playing, two elephants, and a daredevil on a high wire.

In the fourth circus ring, my sister saw with me four aerialists zooming, three monkeys playing, two elephants, and a daredevil on a high wire.

In the fifth circus ring, my sister saw with me five dogs a-barking, four aerialists zooming, three monkeys playing, two elephants, and a daredevil on a high wire.

In the sixth circus ring, my sister saw with me six acrobats, five dogs a-barking, four aerialists zooming, three monkeys playing, two elephants, and a daredevil on a high wire.

In the seventh circus ring, my sister saw with me seven clowns a-clowning, six acrobats, five dogs a-barking, four aerialists zooming, three monkeys playing, two elephants, and a daredevil on a high wire.

706 707 708 709 710

In the eighth circus ring, my sister saw with me eight bears performing, seven clowns a-clowning, six acrobats, five dogs a-barking, four aerialists zooming, three monkeys playing, two elephants, and a daredevil on a high wire.

ADAPTING CHARTS

Charts are very adaptable. They can be enlarged by repeating more of the design or reduced by omitting part of the pattern. A small section of the pattern can be adapted to make a small item such as a pincushion or glasses case. It is worth experimenting by combining or changing the charts and patterns. Also, it is fun to work out new color combinations.

USING A ROLLER FRAME

To produce a finished canvas with a good even tension and neat stitches, use a roller frame. A roller frame makes it easy to use the correct method of stitching, with one hand feeding the needle up through the canvas and the other returning it down to form the stitch. Although this is not an essential piece of equipment, it helps keep the canvas evenly stretched. A roller frame is especially useful when working designs with a variety of stitches which are more likely to distort the canvas.

Canvases which have been stitched without a frame or where the stitches are worked in one movement from the front with one hand are more likely to be badly distorted and difficult to block. Round embroidery hoops distort the canvas where the two rings lock together and damage worked stitches.

The frame should be at least as wide as the width of your canvas; canvas length can be accommodated by rolling each end around the rollers.

Find and mark the center of the canvas at the top and bottom; mark the center point of the webbing on each of the two rollers. Match the center points and stitch the canvas to the webbing on the top and bottom roller, working outward from the center to each side so the canvas is held firmly to the webbing. Roll up the canvas so that the area to be worked is held tightly between the rollers, then tighten the screws on the side pieces. The canvas is now ready to be worked.

HOW TO MAKE A TEMPLATE

For an unusual shape, such as a piece of upholstered furniture, you will need to make a template. Use it to determine the quantities of yarn and size of canvas that will be required. If the furniture to be covered needs reupholstering, have this done before the template is made or allow for the size of new padding. A professional can make a template for you and can upholster the finished work onto the furniture.

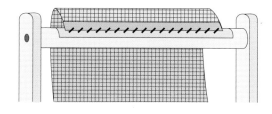

Stitch canvas to webbing, matching the center of the canvas to the center of the webbing.

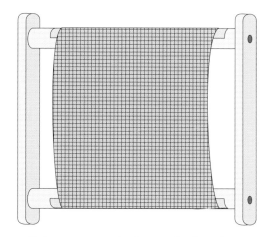

Roll the canvas onto the frame and tighten the screws ready for work.

To make a template, use a piece of muslin, old sheeting, or lining fabric which is larger than the article to be upholstered. Find the center lines of the cloth by folding the fabric in both directions and marking the horizontal and vertical lines with a pencil. Measure and find the center of the item of furniture to be upholstered and lay the piece of marked fabric onto it, matching the two centers. Secure the fabric to the furniture with large basting stitches or pins. Use a pencil to mark the fabric; draw around the outside edge of the area to be worked, adding an allowance for an unworked area to be tucked in underneath – there should be at least 2in (5cm) allowance all around.

Find the center of the canvas by folding in half in both directions and marking the horizontal and vertical lines with a basting thread, then match the center lines of the template to the center of the canvas. Mark the template pattern onto the canvas using a bright-colored thread and basting stitches. Keep the template in case the pattern needs adjusting when finished. Do not cut the canvas until after the stitching has been completed and the piece has been blocked back into shape.

BEADS

The 2mm glass seed beads used in the beadwork chapter are produced specially for embroidery by the US company Mill Hill Beads. They are supplied to stores all over the world and are widely available in both craft and needlework shops. The beadwork projects use a double canvas, which is strong enough to hold the beads in place and provides a good base for the tent-stitch background. The beads are applied using a fine needle and strong cotton thread (see page 124).

Chapter One

REPEATING PATTERNS

A NYBODY who has done even the smallest amount of needle-point will have accumulated some leftover yarns. The more designs you work, the more yarn you collect; most needleworkers have amassed many colors. The simple repeating patterns in this chapter are an excellent way of using up these spare yarns.

Among my collection of fragments of half-worked sample patterns, there are several which I have copied from pillows, footstools, or chairs in friends' houses. Most of these patterns have been passed down through families by mothers, mothers-in-law, and aunts.

Several of the patterns in this chapter are designed for using up odd scraps of different colored yarns. All the patterns use simple stitches; the excitement and interest lies in choosing and mixing the colors for each small part. Find a piece of furniture which might need reupholstering or stitch something smaller like a glasses case, pincushion, or small needlecase.

All the patterns were worked on a mono de luxe canvas, 12 holes to the inch (46 holes/10cm), in antique color for darker yarns or white for the paler yarns. Tapestry wool was used to work the stitches.

PROJECT ONE

Queen Mary's
Tree Pillow

This design was allegedly first worked by Mary Queen of Scots on the corner of a hand-kerchief, using a strand of her red hair for thread, while she was in prison at Fotheringhay Castle. An example of this pattern also turned up among some sample pieces from a Mrs. Evershed, who ran a shop in London's South Molton Street between 1895 and the 1950s. Many of Mrs. Evershed's samples and patterns are still used as inspiration for modern designs. Customers will borrow the exquisitely worked samples to copy and adapt onto canvas using their own colors.

This design is worked in tent stitch with the border in straight gobelin. (For stitch instructions, see pages 123–124.) Each line on the chart represents one thread of canvas.

SIZE 13 × 11in (33 × 28cm)

MATERIALS 17 × 15in (43 × 38cm) mono de luxe antique canvas, 12 holes to the inch (46 holes/10cm), or a piece of canvas 4in (10cm) larger than the area to be worked
Size 18 tapestry needle

TAPESTRY WOOL
Appleton, use 1 strand throughout
Paternayan, use 2 strands throughout

	Suggested color combinations:	Appleton	Paternayan
1	Bright China Blue	741	564
	Bright China Blue	743	561
2	Dull Rose Pink	145	911
	Rose Pink	754	913
3	Mauve	603	323
	Rose Pink	751	946

		Appleton	Paternayan	
4	Heraldic Gold	843	733	
	Bright Yellow	551	773	
5	Flame Red	206	871	
	Coral	863	862	
6	Honeysuckle	696	740	
	Honeysuckle	694	733	
7	Flame Red	205	872	
	Flamingo	621	835	
8	Mid Blue	155	533	
	Mid Blue	153	514	
9	Autumn Yellow	474	725	
	Autumn Yellow	472	703	
10	Bright Rose Pink	945	904	
	Bright Rose Pink	941	934	
11	Grass Green	253	693	
	Gray Green	351	605	
12	Dull Rose Pink	622	834	
	Bright Rose Pink	943	932	
Trellis				
	Grass Green	256	650	½ hank
Background				
	Chocolate	181	475	2 hanks
Border				
	Heraldic Gold	843	733	½ hank
	Turquoise	522	523	½ hank
	Mid Blue	155	533	½ hank

Quantities are for the project using Appleton yarns

METHOD

1 Find the center of the canvas by folding in half in both directions and marking the horizontal and vertical lines with a basting thread.

2 Following the color code, center the pattern and work the first tree motif in tent stitch as indicated on the chart. Work the green trellis around the trees in tent stitch and fill in the background as the work progresses.

3 When the central pattern is complete, work the outside border in gobelin. The first row is worked over two threads of canvas. The next two rows are worked over three threads of canvas.

4 To finish as a throw pillow, see instructions page 119.

OPPOSITE AND RIGHT A variety of colors in different combinations used with a simple pattern has produced this pretty Queen Mary's Tree Pillow.

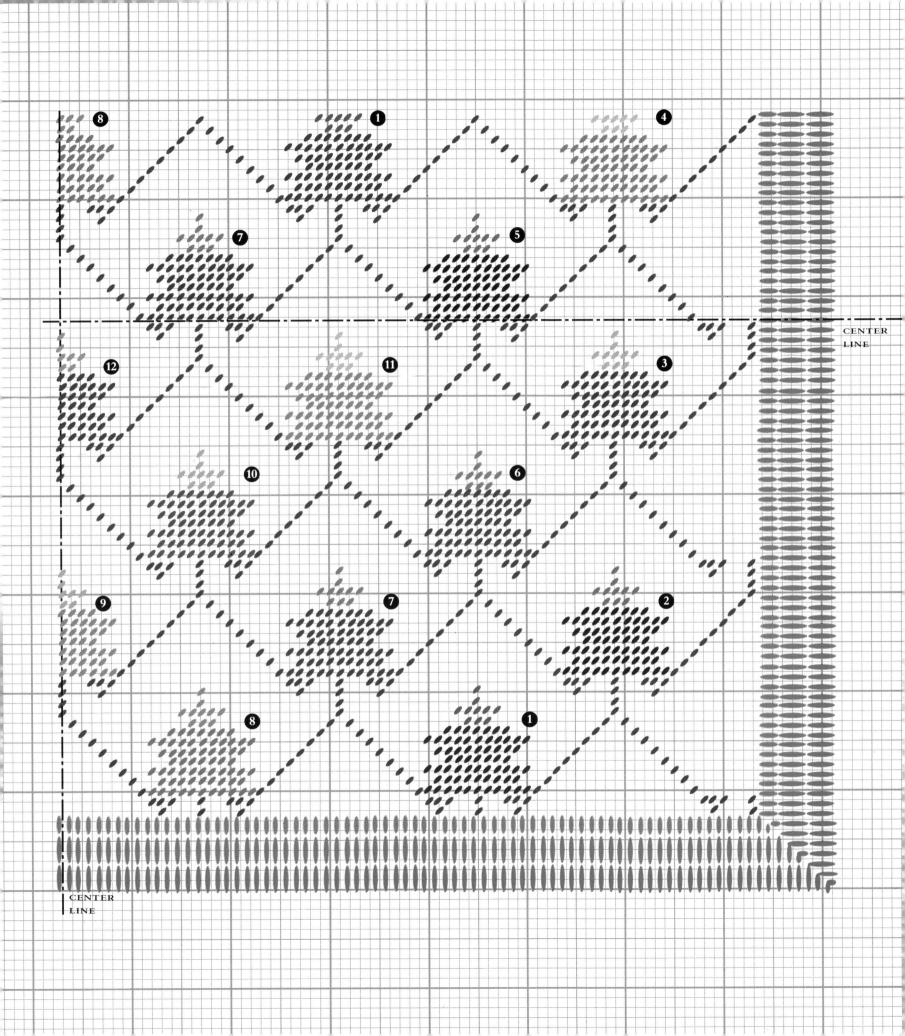

CARNATION PATTERN NEEDLECASE

Through the centuries, the carnation has been a popular motif. In early embroidery, flowers were associated with Christian virtues, and each had a symbolic meaning. The carnation, or dianthus (divine flower), represented love and affection.

There is a pleasing feel about this motif, and the bright colors make a clear and attractive design. Extend the design to any size required by adding more motifs, always keeping the count of the pattern correct. This design is worked in tent stitch throughout. (For stitch instructions see page 124.) Each square on the chart represents one stitch on the canvas.

SIZE Needlecase 5 × 6½in (13 × 16cm) or the pattern can be adapted to fit any size

MATERIALS 9 × 10½in (23 × 27cm) mono de luxe antique canvas, 12 holes to the inch (46 holes/10cm), or no less than 4in (10cm) larger than the finished design size
Size 18 tapestry needle

TAPESTRY WOOL

Appleton, use 1 strand throughout
Paternayan, use 2 strands throughout

	Appleton	Paternayan	
Bright Peacock	832	662	½ hank
Flamingo	626	830	½ hank
Scarlet	502	841	1 skein
Scarlet	504	950	½ hank
Background			
Pastel	877	948	1 hank

Quantities are for the project using Appleton yarns

METHOD

1 Find the center of the canvas by folding in half in both directions and marking the horizontal and vertical lines with a basting thread.

2 Count from the center of the chart and start by working the first carnation nearest the center. Work the rest of the pattern following the chart. Complete the border and then fill in the background.

3 To finish the needlecase, see instructions on page 120.

ABOVE The Carnation Pattern Needlecase uses a beautiful combination of scarlets and flamingo, with a cream background.

CENTER LINE

CENTER LINE

START HERE

FOLD HERE

832/662

626/830

502/841

504/950

877/948 *(background)*

19

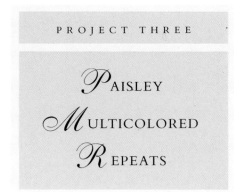

PAISLEY MULTICOLORED REPEATS

This deceptively simple design is based on motifs found in paisley textiles. I found the original pattern in an old junk shop and realized that it would be ideal for using up leftover pieces of yarn. There are more than 200 different colors used on the chair shown in the photograph.

The combination and positioning of the colors in this pattern was an exciting exercise. The blue background color helped to link and combine the motifs, resulting in a bright and cheerful design. If this pattern is used for upholstering a piece of furniture, you will need to make a template (page 11). If you want to make it into a chair cover as shown, you might decide to have it finished professionally.

The design is worked in tent stitch throughout. (For stitch instructions see page 124.) Each square on the chart represents one stitch on the canvas.

SIZE Can be adapted to fit any size

MATERIALS Mono de luxe antique canvas, 12 holes to the inch (46 holes/10cm), at least 4in (10cm) larger than the finished area
Size 18 tapestry needle

TAPESTRY WOOL
Appleton, use 1 strand throughout
Paternayan, use 2 strands throughout

	Appleton	Paternayan
Any assorted colors		
Background		
Dull China Blue	925	210

Quantities are for the project using Appleton yarns

METHOD

1 Find the center of the canvas by folding in half in both directions and marking the horizontal and vertical lines with a basting thread.

2 If a template is being used, match the center of the template with the center of the canvas, making sure that all vertical and horizontal lines match and correspond with the threads of canvas. Using bright-colored thread, baste a line on the canvas to mark the outline.

3 Sort your yarns into bundles of roughly matching colors. Two colors are used for each paisley shape. Each outside row should be worked in a color that will contrast with your background color so that the shape stands out.

4 Work the pattern from the center, matching the center point of the first paisley pattern with the center of the canvas as indicated on the chart. Complete a small section of pattern, then fill in the background around that area, rather than leaving all the background until the end.

5 Work to the template basting line or to your measurements, adjusting if necessary.

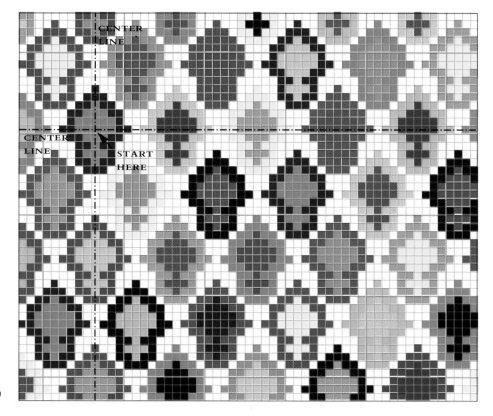

RIGHT In the Paisley Multicolored Repeats, the strong vibrant colors of many tapestry wools are worked together to produce a strong yet classic design used here to upholster a chair.

Rosebud Seat Cover

These little rosebuds were copied from a small design found among some samples discovered in an old wickerwork basket a few years ago. It contained examples of every conceivable exercise in the art of darning, from the invisible mending of holes in knitwear and the patching and darning of wool blankets and sheets and sprigged cotton voiles to turning hems and finishing seams. Among all these exercises were samples of Berlin woolwork and repeated patterns for more leisurely sewing.

This delightfully simple pattern is easy to work and has a very French feel to it. Use it to experiment with different colors. It is a useful pattern for odd pieces of embroidery needed to fit difficult shapes. If it is used for seat covers or to upholster a piece of furniture, you will need to make a template (page 11).

The design is worked in cross stitch and filled in with a tent stitch background. (For stitch instructions see pages 122–124.) Each line on the chart represents one thread of canvas.

MATERIALS Mono de luxe white canvas, 12 holes to the inch (46 holes/10cm), 4in (10cm) larger than the area to be worked
Size 18 tapestry needle
For a seat cover size 13 × 13½in (33 × 34cm):

TAPESTRY WOOL

Appleton, use 1 strand throughout
Paternayan, use 2 strands throughout

	Appleton	Paternayan	
Flame	202	406	½ hank
Bright Terracotta	223	923	½ hank
Grass Green	253	693	½ hank
Background			
White	991	261	2½ hanks

Quantities are for the project using Appleton yarns

METHOD

1 Find the center of the canvas by folding in half in both directions and marking the horizontal and vertical fold lines with a basting thread.

2 If a template is being used, match the center of the template with the center of the canvas, making sure that all vertical and horizontal lines

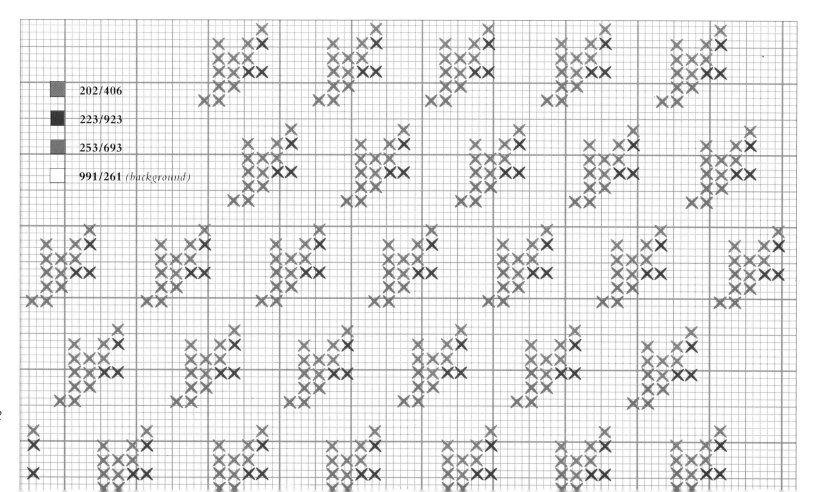

	202/406
	223/923
	253/693
	991/261 *(background)*

match and correspond to the threads of canvas. Using a bright-colored thread, baste a line on the canvas around the edge of the template to mark the outline and keep the template for reference.

3 Center the pattern and begin the embroidery by working the rosebud motifs in cross stitch. Fill in the background in tent stitch.

4 Work to the finish line, or match to the template basting line or your measurements, adjusting if necessary.

5 To finish the seat cover, see page 121.

The rosebud design with its simple cross stitches makes an ideal chair seat cover.

Sprigged Rose Tiebacks

This pretty rose pattern was discovered among some old samples given to me several years ago. The clever placing of the roses across the canvas gives a pleasing effect and would work well for a chair seat, tieback, or footstool. Worked here in pastel colors to give a soft and subtle look, the design would work just as well in stronger colors with a dark background. The design is worked in tent stitch throughout. (For stitch instructions see page 124.) Each square on the chart represents one stitch on the canvas.

SIZE Each tieback is 23½in (60cm) long and 4in (10cm) wide or the pattern can be used for any size

MATERIALS 28½ × 8in (72 × 20cm) mono de luxe white canvas, 12 holes to the inch (46 holes/10cm), or a piece of canvas 4in (10cm) larger than the area to be worked for each tieback

Size 18 tapestry needle

OPPOSITE The Sprigged Rose Tiebacks use a simple pattern, worked across the canvas in tent stitch.

TAPESTRY WOOL

Appleton, use 1 strand throughout
Paternayan, use 2 strands throughout

	Appleton	Paternayan	
Rose Pink	756	932	¼ hank
Rose Pink	754	913	¾ hank
Rose Pink	752	945	½ hank
Gray Green	355	603	¾ hank
Background			
White	991	261	2 hanks

Quantities are for the project using Appleton yarns

METHOD

1 Find the center of the canvas by folding in half in both directions and marking the horizontal and vertical lines with a basting thread.

2 Start by working the center rose flower in tent stitch as indicated on the chart. Make sure the pattern is correctly positioned and allow for hemming the edges.

3 Fill in the background as the work progresses.

4 To finish the tiebacks, see instructions on page 120.

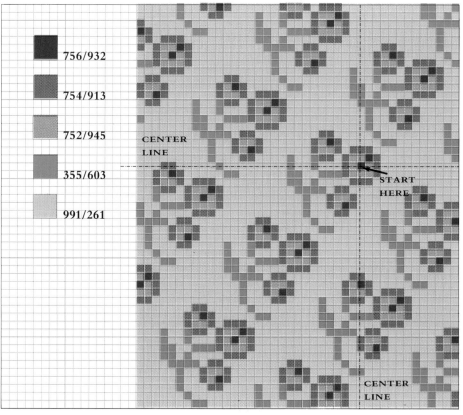

■	756/932
■	754/913
■	752/945
■	355/603
■	991/261

CENTER LINE

START HERE

CENTER LINE

PATCHWORK BLOCKS

Reminiscent of the shapes used in patchwork, this simple pattern would be easy for a beginner. The vivid colors of the patchwork blocks have been subdued by a brown background, while the thoughtful placing of these combinations has produced an exciting mix. The design would work equally well using any other bright color combination. Pale pastel colors would give a soft muted look, and a different textured finish could be achieved by using stranded floss in the center of each block.

If this pattern is used for a footstool cover or to upholster a piece of furniture, you will need to make a template (page 11).

The design is worked in tent stitch throughout. (For stitch instructions, see page 124.) Each square on the chart represents one stitch on the canvas.

SIZE Can be adapted to fit any size

MATERIALS Mono de luxe antique canvas, 12 holes to the inch (46 holes/10cm), 4in (10cm) larger than the area to be worked
Size 18 tapestry needle

OPPOSITE The diamonds of the Patchwork Blocks design have been worked in bright jewel colors to upholster this footstool.

TAPESTRY WOOL

Appleton, use I strand throughout
Paternayan, use 2 strands throughout

	Appleton	Paternayan
Suggested color combinations:		
Rose Pink	755	932
Rose Pink	757	902
Royal Blue	822	542
Bright China Blue	744	562
Early English Green	546	691
Early English Green	544	692
Heraldic Gold	844	714
Heraldic Gold	842	734
Centers		
White	992	263
Background		
Brown Grounding	581	470

Quantities are for the project using Appleton yarns

METHOD

1 Find the center of the canvas by folding in half in both directions and marking the horizontal and vertical lines with a basting thread.

2 If a template is used, match the center of the template to the center of the canvas, making sure that all vertical and horizontal lines match and correspond with the threads of canvas.

3 Using a brightly colored thread, baste a line on the canvas around the edge of the template to mark the outline.

4 Center the pattern and start by working the brown outline to each diamond.

5 Fill in each pattern with the relative colors before moving on to the next area.

6 Only work one color at a time to avoid tangling threads on the back of the work.

7 Work to the template basting line or to your measurements, adjusting if necessary.

755/932

757/902

822/542

744/562

546/691

544/692

844/714

842/734

992/263 *(center)*

581/470 *(background)*

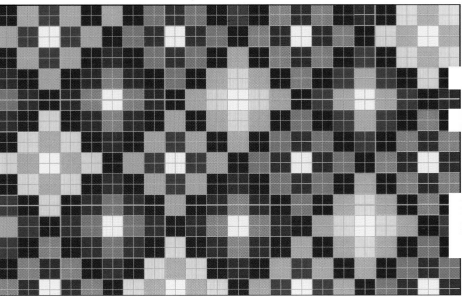

Chapter Two

SAMPLERS

*M*AKING *samplers is an ancient craft. Even the earliest known examples, found in Egyptian burial tombs, show different patterns, stitches, and techniques worked on fabric.*

Before pattern books were available, samplers were the only means of recording stitches and patterns. Beginners used samplers to learn how the stitches were worked; then they copied them as a means of practicing the stitches. Inspiration for the designs came from woodcuts, illustrated manuscripts, or even herbals. The threads were silks and fine wools dyed naturally.

By the middle of the sixteenth century, domestic embroidery was growing in popularity, and needlework occupied a great part of a lady's day. Household linens and furnishings were extensively decorated, while clothes were richly embroidered and trimmed with beautiful laces. Making samplers was an easy way of recording new patterns so that they could be used again and passed on to others. Toward the end of the century, pattern books were being produced commercially, and the popular patterns which appeared in many different samplers of this period can be traced back to these.

A book first published in 1624, titled A Shole-house for the Needle *by Richard Shorleyker, contained many small motifs of fruit, birds, fish and flowers. Lace patterns with details of other embroidery were also included. Many of the small motifs from this book are still in use today.*

In the eighteenth century, more natural flower designs, found on the printed textiles of that period, were interpreted onto samplers. Pattern books were expensive, and professionally drawn samplers became a cheaper way of producing these designs; the outline of the pattern was drawn onto the fabric ready for working (like our printed designs today). Map samplers, showing different counties, were done in the same way. Many of those which have survived were obviously commercially produced, identical except for the occasional small personal touch such as a pretty flower border or the stitcher's name and home village marked on the map.

Printed patterns on linen and canvas became popular in the nineteenth century. There was also an increase in the production of pattern books with detailed instructions, so samplers were no longer necessary to record techniques and patterns. At this time Berlin woolwork became very fashionable, worked from hand-colored or printed charts on squared paper. Samplers were, however, still being made by the Victorians, possibly to make confusing charts easier to understand and copy.

Today, interest in samplers has seen something of a revival. Antique needlework samplers have become collectors' items. They can be expensive to buy, but they are a wonderful source of ideas for new designs. A sampler is fun to sew, makes a popular gift, and looks very decorative when framed and hung on the wall.

ALPHABET SAMPLER

Working a sampler was an essential part of a Victorian girl's education, as it would teach her techniques and stitches that would be useful after her marriage to decorate both her home and her clothes. Embroidery was also a leisure pursuit for ladies.

This design is typical of the Berlin woolwork samplers of the Victorian era, which would have a border of little rosebuds or carnations, small motifs, a pious verse, and an alphabet with the date and age of the child working it. The finished sampler would then be framed and hung on the wall by the proud parents. The delightfully simple alphabet has a typical rosebud border and rosebuds intertwining through the letters. It could be made into a pillow or framed as a picture.

This design uses only tent stitch, so it would be suitable for a beginner to work. (For stitch instructions see page 124.) Each square on the chart represents one stitch.

SIZE 15½ × 12½in (39 × 32cm)

MATERIALS 20 × 17in (51 × 43cm) mono de luxe antique canvas, 14 holes to the inch (56 holes/10cm)

Graph paper large enough to work out your chosen initials

Size 20 tapestry needle

CREWEL WOOL

Appleton, use 3 strands throughout
Paternayan, use 2 strands throughout

	Appleton	Paternayan	
Rose Pink	754	913	¼ hank
Rose Pink	752	945	¼ hank
Sea Green	402	612	½ hank
Pastel	874	624	¼ hank
Heraldic Gold	841	704	¾ hank
Background			
Bright Peacock	835	660	3 hanks

Quantities are for the project using Appleton yarns

METHOD

1 Find the center of the canvas by folding in half in both directions and marking the horizontal and vertical lines with a basting thread.

2 Following the color code and stitch chart, start in the center. Work the letters first, using tent stitch. Fill in the background as work progresses, also using tent stitch.

3 To work the border, start from the center line and work the first flower shown on the chart, then complete the remainder of the border.

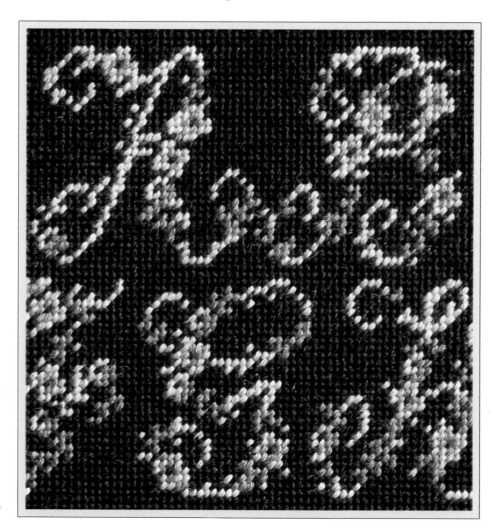

RIGHT The classic Alphabet Sampler combines roses with letters from a traditional alphabet, all worked in one simple stitch.

754/913

752/945

402/612

874/624

841/704

835/660 *(background)*

STAR
HERE

CENTER LINE

START
BORDER
HERE

Noah's Ark

The story of Noah is the theme of this sampler, which has been designed with a child's room in mind. The animals around the border and the traditional lettering in the center make a pleasing picture to hang on the wall of a playroom or nursery. The sampler could be adapted to give a child's name and date of birth instead of the numbers, while a longer message could replace the alphabet.

This design uses four easy textured stitches: tent, cross, and straight and slanting gobelin, so it would be suitable for a beginner. (For stitch instructions see pages 122–124.) Each line on the chart represents one thread of canvas.

This lovely sampler with its depiction of Noah's Ark would be fun to work as a gift for a child.

SIZE 10½ × 14½in (27 × 37cm)

MATERIALS 15 × 19in (38 × 48cm) mono de luxe antique canvas, 14 holes to the inch (56 holes/10cm)

Graph paper large enough to work out your chosen initials

Size 20 tapestry needle

CREWEL WOOL

Appleton, use 3 strands throughout
Paternayan, use 2 strands throughout

	Appleton	Paternayan	
Brown Grounding	586	421	½ hank
Iron Gray	963	202	¼ hank
White	991	261	¼ hank
Bright Terracotta	224	931	¼ hank
Honeysuckle	698	412	1 skein
Honeysuckle	695	732	1 skein
Sea Green	402	612	¼ hank
Bright China Blue	745	560	1 skein
Rose Pink	751	946	1 skein
Background			
Honeysuckle	691	444	2½ hanks

Quantities are for the project using Appleton yarns

METHOD

1 Find the center of the canvas by folding in half in both directions. Mark the horizontal and vertical fold lines with a basting thread.

2 Following the color code and the stitch chart, start in the center. Work all the alphabet letters, using cross stitch. Fill in the background with tent stitch as work progresses.

3 Work the ark below the letters using tent, slanting gobelin, and cross stitch. Work the waves in cross stitch and the numbers in tent stitch, fill in the background around them with tent stitch.

4 The entire animal border is worked in tent stitch. Start from the horizontal center line and work the first elephant. Then continue working to complete all the animals, following the color code and the stitch chart.

5 Complete the design by filling in the background around the border.

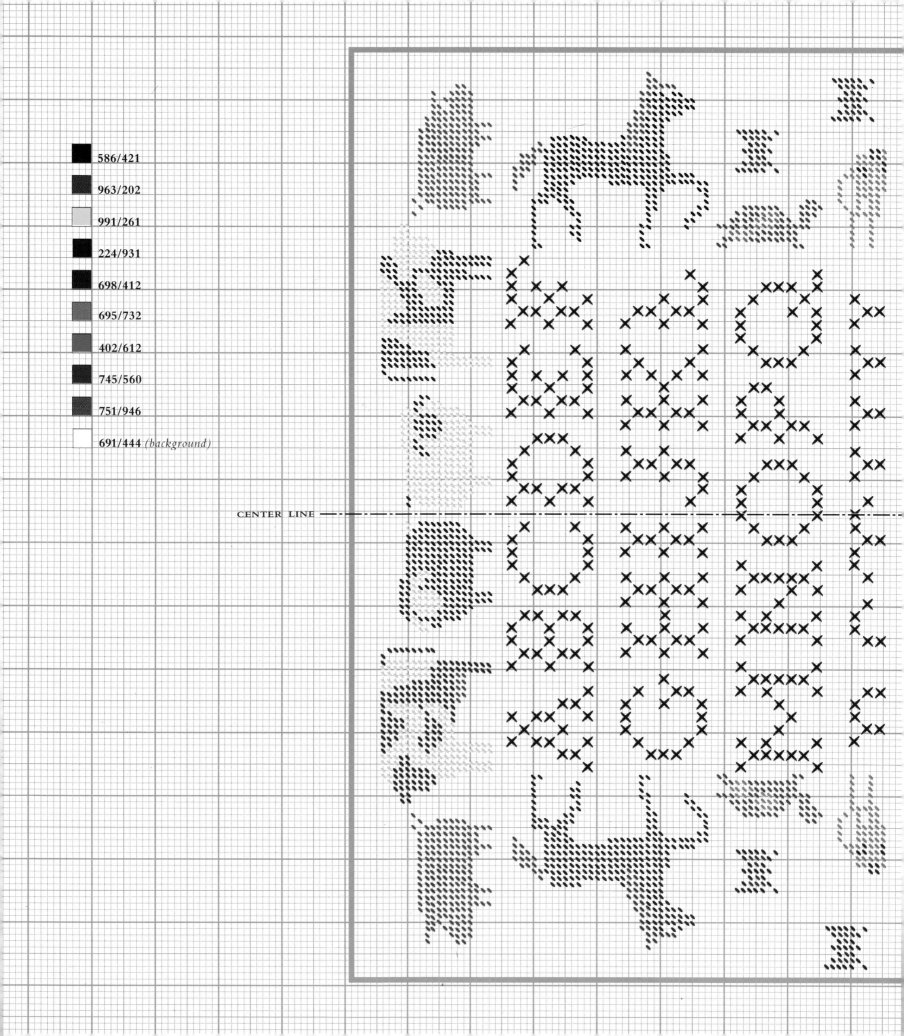

586/421

963/202

991/261

224/931

698/412

695/732

402/612

745/560

751/946

691/444 *(background)*

CENTER LINE

CENTER LINE

START
HERE

CENTER
LINE

VICTORIAN CROSS STITCH SAMPLER

Berlin woolwork was a very distinctive sewing fashion of the Victorian era. Designs were worked on charts using wools imported from Germany and girls were taught at home, working their samplers under the strict eye of a governess. The popular samplers often had alphabets and numbers in cross stitch, with little motifs of birds, animals, and flowers. (Many such designs could also be used in tiny stitches to mark linen.) Girls were also instructed in all the techniques for making and mending clothes, and many worked samplers to practice the necessary neatness and precision.

The double canvas used for this sampler is typical of the canvas used in the latter part of the nineteenth century, and the colors capture the feel and style of Berlin woolwork with a traditional unworked background.

This sampler uses only cross stitch in one strand of crewel wool throughout. The background has not been filled in, but could be worked with tent stitch (3 strands). (For stitch instructions see pages 122–124.) Each square on the chart represents one stitch on the canvas.

OPPOSITE The Victorian Cross Stitch Sampler captures the feel and style of Berlin woolwork.

SIZE 23¾ × 17½in (60 × 44cm)

MATERIALS 28 × 22in (70 × 55cm) double-thread antique-brown canvas, 14 holes to the inch (56 holes/10cm)
Graph paper
Size 20 tapestry needle

CREWEL WOOL

Appleton, use 1 strand throughout
Paternayan, use 1 strand throughout

	Appleton	Paternayan	
Autumn Yellow	472	703	½ hank
Autumn Yellow	475	723	¼ hank
Autumn Yellow	478	721	¼ hank
Rose Pink	754	913	½ hank
Rose Pink	756	932	½ hank
Early English Green	542	653	½ hank
Early English Green	544	692	1½ hanks
Early English Green	545	691	2½ hanks

Quantities are for the project using Appleton yarns

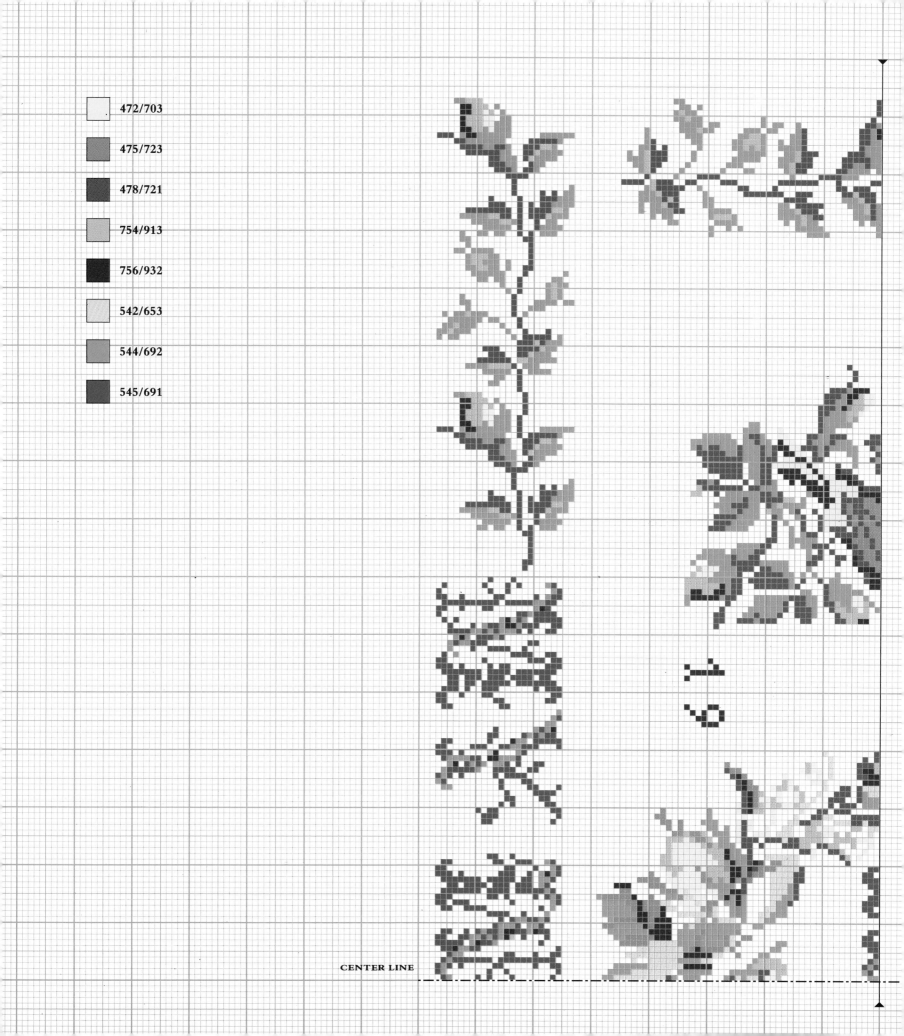

472/703

475/723

478/721

754/913

756/932

542/653

544/692

545/691

CENTER LINE

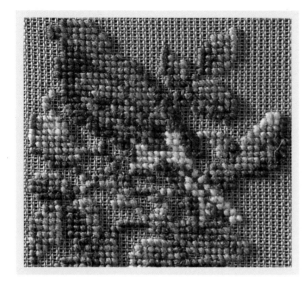

METHOD

1 Find the center of the canvas by folding in half in both directions and marking the horizontal and vertical lines with a basting thread.

2 Following color code and stitch chart, start in the center and work the first leaf of the central garland. Because the background of this sampler is not worked, it is important to take care of any trailing threads. All starting and ending threads should be darned into the back of previously worked stitches, and all thread ends should be trimmed very short to keep the back of the embroidery as neat as possible.

3 Work the central motif and the birds on each side, omitting the initials, then work the remaining motifs and the alphabet.

4 To work the chosen initials in the central motif, you will need a piece of graph paper, pencil, and eraser. Fill in spaces on graph paper with the initials you want to use. When letters and spaces are correct, find the center of the design on the graph paper. Copy and stitch onto canvas using colors from the color key.

5 To work the border, start from the center line, following color code and stitch chart.

CENTER

START HERE

CENTER LINE

House AND Garden Sampler

This design of a country house set in gardens with countryside in the background and surrounded by a border of strawberries uses traditional sampler images. Samplers would often tell a story and portray an embroidered stately home with family crests and household pets. Sometimes figures appear among the rows of classic borders and patterns, making personal mementoes to be passed down through the family.

Many of these samplers were divided into thirds. In the top section would be a pious verse or alphabet, in the middle a house or scene, then at the bottom a garden with animals, birds, and butterflies. The sections would be divided by two decorative borders and the whole sampler would be framed with a traditional floral border. A variety of stitches and different techniques could be incorporated.

This sampler can be adapted to incorporate dates and initials or a message. There is space at the top in the sky on each side of the house for initials and dates; a message could be worked where the alphabet is shown.

This sampler uses seven textured stitches: tent, cross, leaf, brick, Scottish variation, straight gobelin, and Hungarian variation. Because so many different stitches are used, it is a good project for an intermediate or advanced needle-worker. (For stitch instructions see pages 122–124.) Each line on the chart represents one thread of canvas.

SIZE 14½ × 12in (37 × 30cm)

MATERIALS 19 × 16in (47 × 40cm) mono de luxe antique canvas, 14 holes to the inch (56 holes/10cm)
Graph paper large enough to work out words, initials, or dates to replace alphabet and numbers, if required
Size 20 tapestry needle

CREWEL WOOL

Appleton, use 3 strands throughout
Paternayan, use 2 strands throughout

	Appleton	Paternayan	
Bright Terracotta	224	931	¾ hank
Honeysuckle	695	732	¼ hank
Honeysuckle (incl. background)	691	444	2¾ hanks
Bright China Blue	743	561	½ hank
Early English Green	545	691	½ hank
Early English Green	543	693	½ hank
White	991	261	¼ hank

Quantities are for the project using Appleton yarns

METHOD

1 Find the center of the canvas by folding in half in both directions and marking the horizontal and vertical lines with a basting thread.

2 Follow the color code and stitch chart to stitch the path up to the house first, starting at the center point.

3 Work the trees and birds on each side of the house and fill in the background in tent stitch as work progresses. Fill in the sky around the house, then work the path on each side of the house. Work the fence, then the flowerbeds.

4 Complete the alphabet, filling in the background as you work.

5 To work the border, find the center line. Follow the color code and the stitch chart and start with a cross stitch. Complete the strawberries and leaves; fill in the background in tent stitch as work progresses.

The traditional House and Garden Sampler could become a cherished family heirloom.

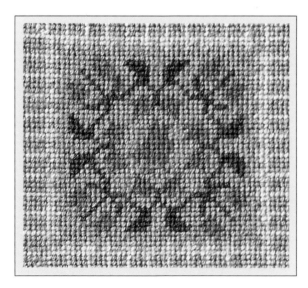

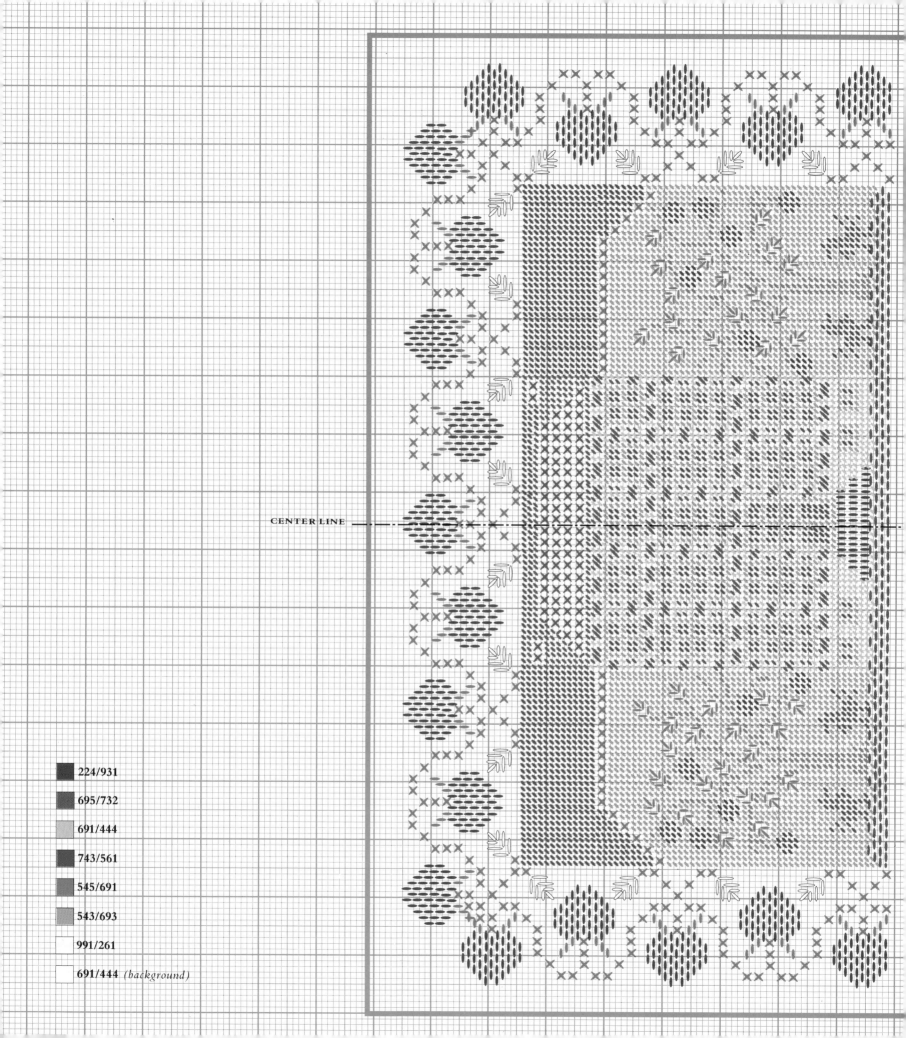

CENTER LINE

224/931

695/732

691/444

743/561

545/691

543/693

991/261

691/444 *(background)*

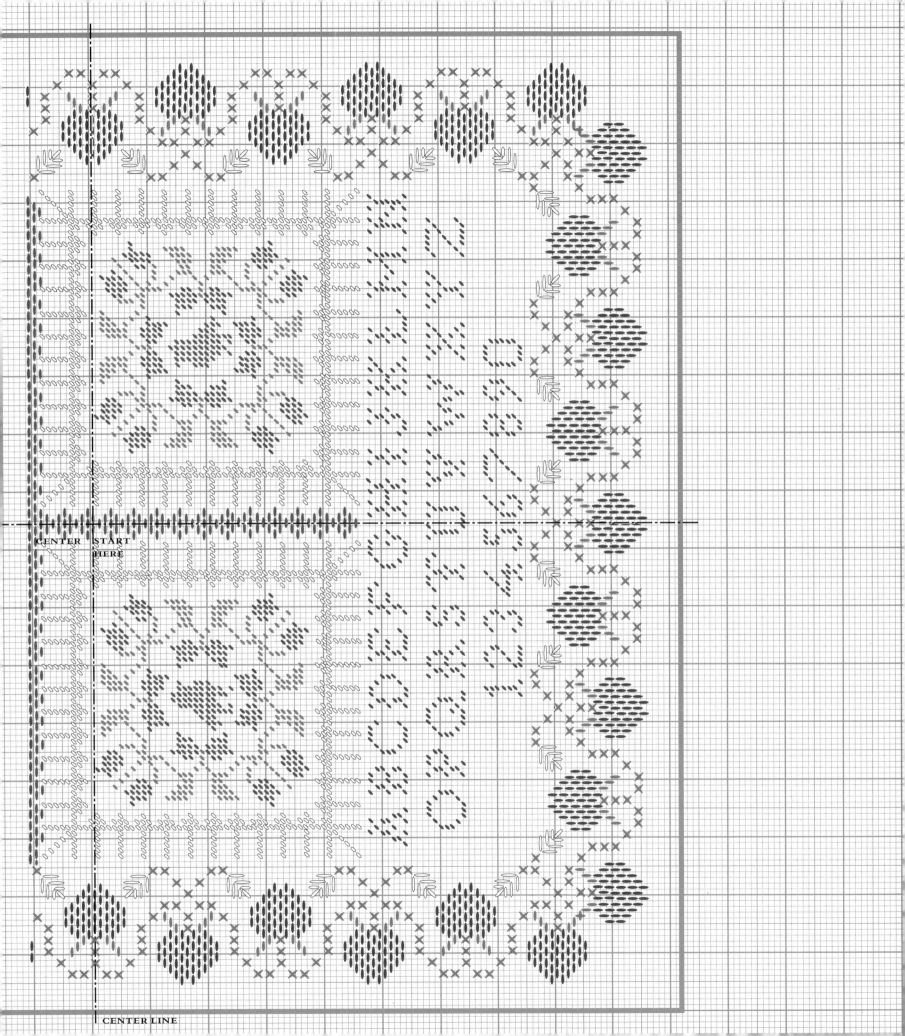

CENTER START
HERE

CENTER LINE

Chapter Three

BEADWORK

*D*ECORATING *jewelry and textiles with beads is an ancient skill. In the Middle East, beadwork was developed into a fine craft, and in medieval times, beads were exported by glassmaking countries such as Italy and France. Elizabethan court portraits show how beads were used in the fifteenth century. Semiprecious stones and seed pearls were expertly sewn onto courtiers' elaborate clothes and enhanced by beautiful gold thread embroidery worked on luxury fabrics, using especially fine needles.*

In the seventeenth century, bead embroidery was used to cover objects like caskets, jewel boxes, belts, and purses, as well as decorate textiles. All forms of embroidery were part of a girl's education, and bead-work techniques were the last stage in this training. A young girl might also be instructed to work a jewel casket with bead-embroidered panels and lid. The patterns and images were often the same as those used on other types of embroidery, as they were frequently taken from the same design books and prints.

As fashions changed, so did the use of beads. Throughout the eighteenth century, increasingly lighter fabrics were used, and since they could not be heavily beaded, beading became simpler. About the same time, smaller and more intricate items such as watch chains, needlecases, and napkin rings were covered in beads.

It is fairly easy to date a piece of bead embroidery by the size of the beads, as they tended to get larger toward the end of the nineteenth century. Beads were applied using a loom, a tambour frame, or with a needle and thread.

The Victorian era saw a revival in needle arts and in the availability of new patterns and supplies. Many magazines published embroidery patterns which combined Victorian woolwork with beads. Sometimes the beads highlighted the design or the whole pattern might be worked in beads, leaving the background to be worked in yarn or stranded cotton. As far as the Victorians were concerned, all manner of household and personal belongings could be decorated with beads: teapot stands, firescreens, valances, mantelpiece covers, mats, belts, suspenders, hats, and throw pillows. Toward the end of the nineteenth century, beads were again used extensively to decorate clothes from day wear to ballgowns, while jet beads were used on mourning clothes.

During the early part of the twentieth century, there was little interest in beading until the Twenties, when beaded cocktail dresses and accessories such as shoes, handbags, and hats became fashionable. Many of these articles have survived and are in family collections.

In this chapter, only glass seed beads are used, stitched with a fine needle and thread on double canvas. The beads are available from specialty needlework and craft stores. The double canvas is strong enough to hold the beads in place and forms a good base for a background worked in crewel yarn. Each bead will lie on the canvas in the opposite direction to the tent stitch background. To prevent twisting threads and to strengthen the yarn, wax the cotton thread. Tent stitch is used to work the design areas. Cross stitch and other textured stitches may be used to frame the work.

BEADED Tudor Pillow

Inspired by images from Tudor and Elizabethan embroideries, this beadwork throw pillow depicts flowers and insects in beads within a gold framework. Sixteenth-century bead embroidery was elaborate and used the finest beads, often made of semiprecious stones and pearls, which were so tiny it is difficult to imagine how they were threaded and sewn onto the fabric. Glass beads imported from Europe were often used on caskets and in embroidered pictures showing Biblical scenes. These scenes were often exquisite collections of small and large animals, insects, castles, rivers and hillocks.

This small pillow is easy to make and uses lots of different colored seed beads with gold metallic thread. The beads are applied onto the design with a diagonal stitch over two close threads of canvas; the background is filled in with tent stitch using three strands of crewel wool over two close threads of canvas. (For beading and stitch instructions, see pages 122–124.) Each line on the chart represents two close threads of canvas.

SIZE 13 × 9in (33 × 23cm)

MATERIALS 17 × 13in (43 × 33cm) double-thread antique canvas, 14 holes to the inch (56 holes/10cm)
Size 9 straw needle for beading
Size 20 tapestry needle
Cotton sewing thread for applying beads
Madeira Braid, Glissen Gloss metallic thread, BR03, 3 spools

The richly beaded Tudor Pillow depicting flowers and insects was inspired by embroideries of the sixteenth century.

CREWEL WOOL

Appleton, use 3 strands throughout
Paternayan, use 2 strands throughout

	Appleton	Paternayan	
Background			
Cornflower Blue	465	540	2 hanks

Quantities are for the project using Appleton yarns

Mill Hill Glass Seed Beads

Victorian Gold	2011	1 pack
Christmas Green	167	3 packs
Christmas Red	165	3 packs
White	479	1 pack
Yellow	128	1 pack
Ice Lilac	2009	1 pack
Robin-Egg Blue	143	1 pack
Satin Blue	2007	1 pack
Mercury	283	1 pack
Tea Rose	2004	1 pack
Pink	145	1 pack
Rainbow	374	1 pack
Iris	252	1 pack
Yellow Cream	2002	1 pack
Violet	206	1 pack
Sapphire	168	1 pack
Emerald	332	1 pack
Cobalt Blue	358	1 pack
Red	968	1 pack

METHOD

1 Find the center of the canvas by folding in half in both directions and marking the horizontal and vertical lines with a basting thread.

2 Start at the center of the chart by working the diamond framework pattern in gold thread, working from the center out. Thread the tapestry needle with a short length of gold thread about 14in (36cm) long; a longer length will fray. Work in cross stitch to complete frames and border before starting the beadwork.

3 Thread the straw needle with a doubled sewing thread and apply the beads, working from the chart to fill the frames with the patterns (see page 124). The beads will lie in the opposite direction to the tent stitch background.

4 Thread the tapestry needle with three strands of yarn and work the background in tent stitch over two close threads of canvas.

5 To finish the pillow, see page 119.

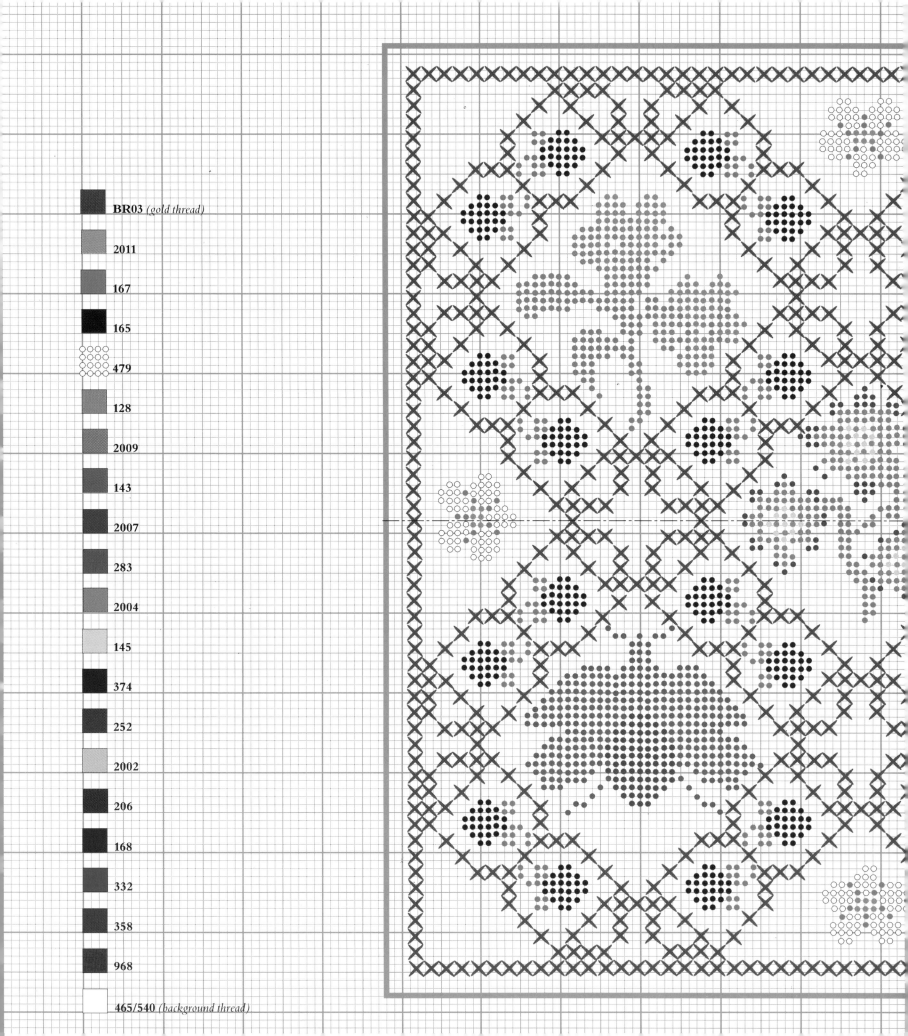

BR03 *(gold thread)*

2011

167

165

479

128

2009

143

2007

283

2004

145

374

252

2002

206

168

332

358

968

465/540 *(background thread)*

CENTER LINE

START HERE

CENTER LINE

BEADED FLORAL WREATH FOOTSTOOL

A traditional combination of intertwining flowers and leaves embroidered with beads. The finished design, used here to upholster a Victorian-style inlaid mahogany footstool, could also be used for a pillow.

17in sq (43cm sq) double-thread antique canvas, 14 holes to the inch (56 holes/10cm)
Size 9 straw needle for beading
Size 20 tapestry needle
Cotton sewing thread for applying beads

CREWEL WOOL
Appleton, use 3 strands throughout
Paternayan, use 2 strands throughout

	Appleton	Paternayan	
Background			
Brown Grounding	585	421	3 hanks

Quantities are for the project using Appleton yarns

Mill Hill Glass Seed Beads

Mercury	283	4 packs
Christmas Green	167	5 packs
Garnet	367	1 pack
Red	968	1 pack
Tea Rose	2004	2 packs
Pink	145	1 pack
Iris	252	1 pack
Ice Lilac	2009	1 pack
Sapphire	168	1 pack
Light Blue	146	1 pack
Ash Mauve	151	1 pack
White	479	1 pack
Tangerine	423	1 pack
Yellow	128	1 pack

This pretty wreath of flowers worked in beads has been designed to fit a round footstool, but the background could easily be squared off for a throw pillow. The design was inspired by Berlin woolwork patterns, which were fashionable throughout the nineteenth century. The beading of these patterns became very popular in the middle of the century, using delicately colored beads made in France. Some designs were very effectively worked in shades of black, gray, and white beads.

This pattern is worked with beads which are applied onto the design with a diagonal stitch over two close threads of canvas; the background is filled in with tent stitch using three strands of yarn over two close threads of canvas. (For beading and stitch instructions, see page 124.) Each square on the chart represents one bead or one tent stitch of the background.

SIZE Finished design size 12½in (32cm). This design can be extended by increasing the background area to fit a larger footstool or made into a square.

METHOD

1 Find the center of the canvas by folding in half in both directions and marking the horizontal and vertical lines with a basting thread. Draw a circle from the center of the canvas to the required size for your footstool using a pencil and then baste around the pencil line.

2 Find the center of the chart and count on the canvas to the first flower to be worked.

3 Thread the straw needle with cotton thread. Using a double thread, apply the beads, working from the first flower. Sew all the beaded parts of the design following the colored beading chart. The beads will lie in the opposite direction to the tent stitch background.

4 Thread the larger tapestry needle with three strands of yarn and work the background.

5 To mount onto a footstool or finish as a throw pillow, see pages 119 and 121.

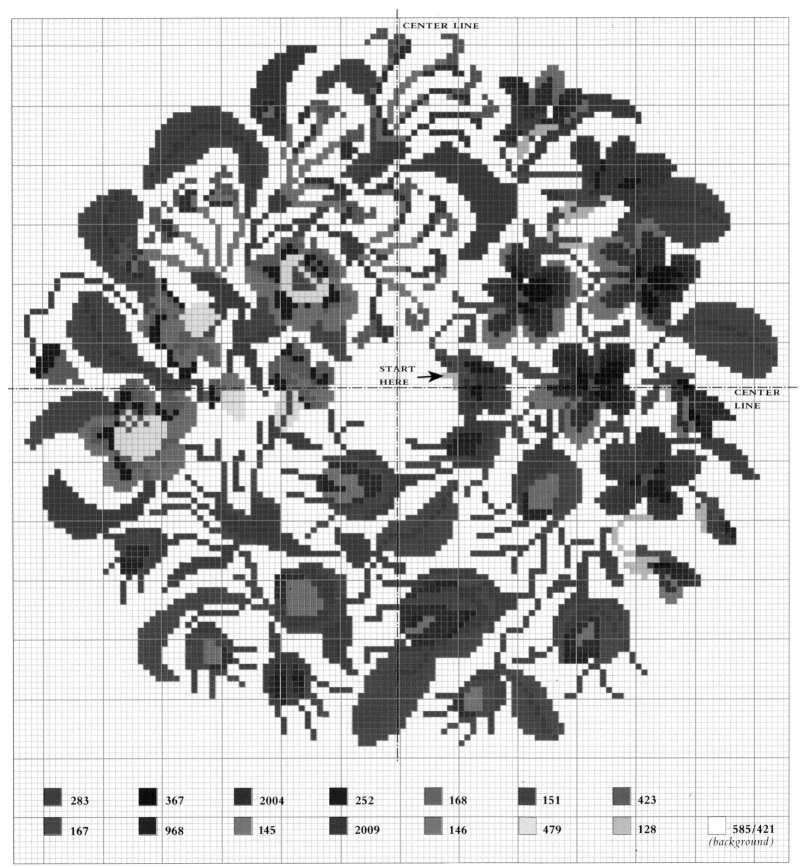

Beaded Rosebud Vest

The design of this vest was influenced by silk embroideries of the seventeenth century. Many fine embroidered vests are still in beautiful condition, both in private and public collections, which suggests that they were highly valued and cared for well.

These seventeenth-century waistcoats were embroidered heavily around the edges, with a spot motif worked all over the background. Here and there the pattern was enhanced by coiled metal threads and small steel sequins; often both the pocket flaps and buttons were worked in the same pattern. Very well-made, fine needles were essential for such fine work.

This vest features flowers and leaves which intertwine around each other as they might grow in a garden. Both the look and feel of this type of design echo textiles and embroideries of the seventeenth century.

This pattern is worked with beads which are applied onto the design with a diagonal stitch over two close threads of canvas, and the background is filled in with tent stitch using three strands of crewel wool over two close threads of canvas.

This project is for reasonably experienced embroiderers and dressmakers. The vest itself can be made from a basic sewing pattern. Most pattern companies have several designs from which to choose. (For beading and stitch instructions, see page 124.) Each square on the canvas represents one bead or one tent stitch of the background.

SIZE To fit medium chest size 36–38in (92–97cm). The size of the waistcoat may be altered and the design of the beaded embroidery adjusted accordingly.

MATERIALS 28 × 35in (70 × 90cm) double-thread antique canvas, 14 holes to the inch (56 holes/10cm)
Size 9 straw needle for beading
Size 20 tapestry needle
Cotton sewing thread for applying beads

OPPOSITE The look and feel of the Beaded Rosebud Vest echo textiles and embroideries of the seventeenth century.

CREWEL WOOL

Appleton, use 3 strands throughout
Paternayan, use 2 strands throughout

	Appleton	Paternayan	
Background			
Rose Pink	759	900	8 hanks

Quantities are for the project using Appleton yarns

Mill Hill Glass Seed Beads

Christmas Green	167	11 packs
Red	968	4 packs

METHOD

1 Center the two fronts of the paper pattern on the canvas and pin. Baste around the outer edge to mark the outline. If the pattern has darts, do not mark them, as they would be too bulky on the finished design, but compensate by taking ¼in (5mm) out of the side seams.

2 Remove the paper pattern and work an inner row of basting to show the seam allowances which will be left unworked.

3 Cut the canvas in half so that each front is a separate piece. Do not cut out the pattern; leave each pattern front as a rectangular piece of canvas so that it can be attached to a frame if necessary.

4 To mark the center of each vest front, fold the canvas in half in both directions and mark horizontal and vertical lines with basting thread.

5 Find the center of the chart and count to the outside edge of the canvas to start the first beaded flower.

6 Thread the straw needle with a doubled cotton thread and apply the beads, working from the first flower. Sew all the beaded areas of the design, following the colored beading chart. The beads will lie in the opposite direction to the tent stitch background.

7 Thread the larger tapestry needle with three strands of yarn and work the background to the inner row of basting thread. Leave the seam allowances unworked.

8 Complete both sides of the vest front.

9 Finish by following the pattern instructions.

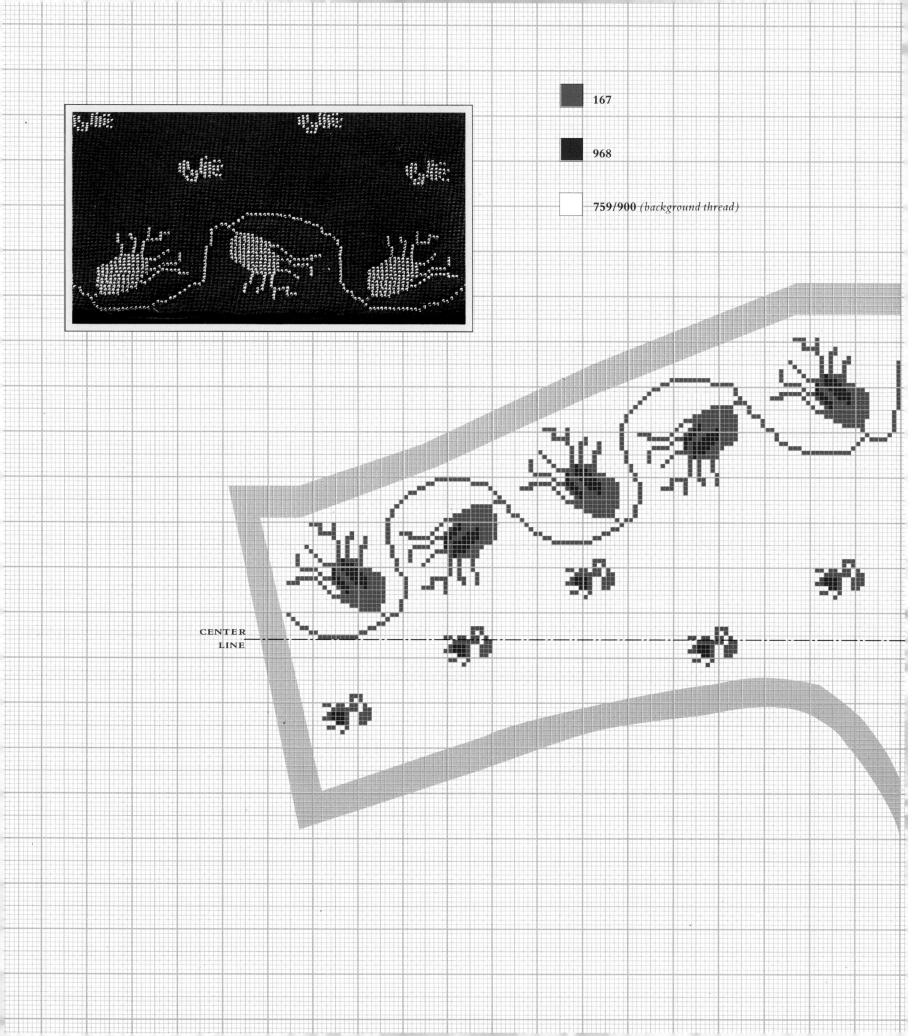

167

968

759/900 *(background thread)*

CENTER
LINE

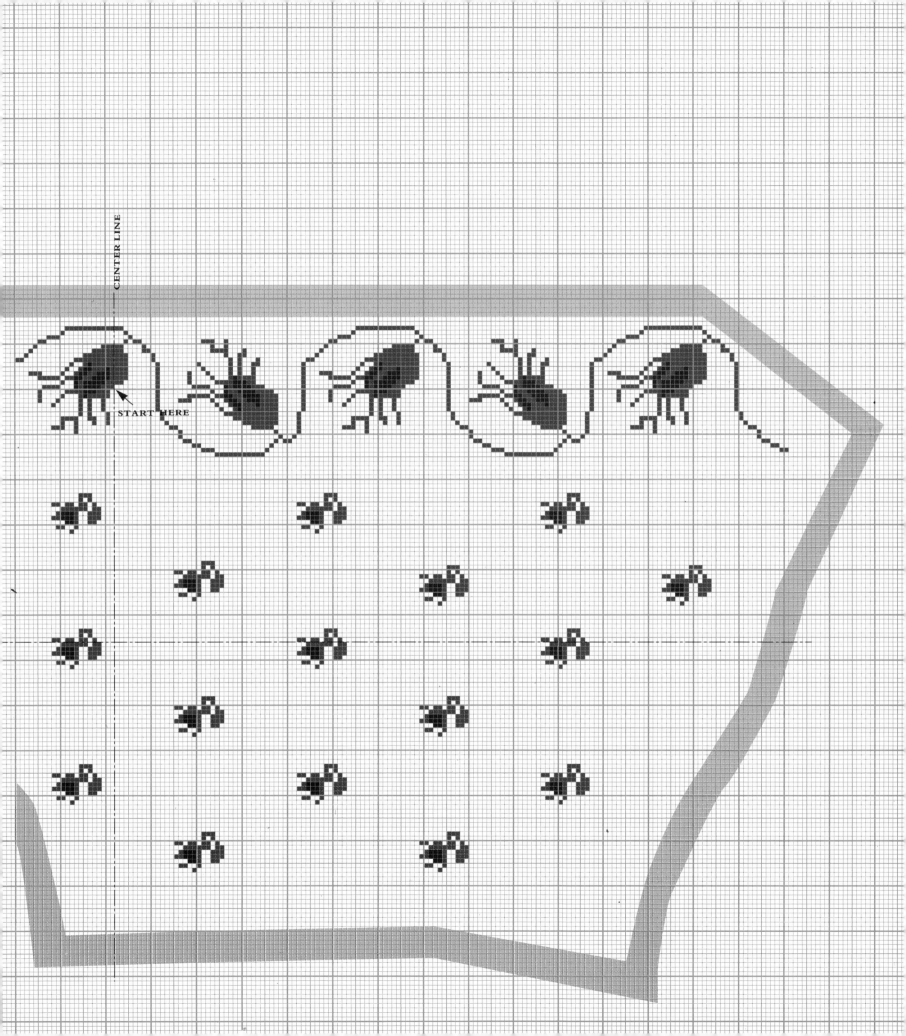

CENTER LINE

START HERE

Beaded Strawberry Glasses Case

The beads on the Beaded
Strawberry Glasses Case
reflect the glowing color of real
strawberries.

The strawberry motif appears through the centuries in all forms of embroidery, particularly samplers – equaled in popularity only by the carnation. Early designs featured the entire plant in paintings, drapes and hangings.

Each square on the chart represents one bead or one tent stitch of the background. For beading and stitch instructions, see page 124.

SIZE 6¾ × 3½in (17 × 9cm)

MATERIALS 18 × 8in (44 × 19cm) double-thread antique canvas, 14 holes to the inch (56 holes/10cm)

Size 9 straw needle for beading
Size 20 tapestry needle
Cotton sewing thread for applying beads
Madeira Braid, Glissen Gloss metallic thread, BR03, 1 spool

CREWEL WOOL

Appleton, use 3 strands throughout
Paternayan, use 2 strands throughout

	Appleton	Paternayan	
Background			
Royal Blue	825	540	I hank

Quantities are for the project using Appleton yarns

Mill Hill Glass Seed Beads		
Yellow	I28	I pack
Christmas Green	I67	I pack
White	479	I pack
Christmas Red	I65	I pack

METHOD

1 Find the center of the canvas by folding in half in both directions and marking the horizontal and vertical lines with a basting thread.

2 Find the center of the chart and count on the canvas to the first strawberry to be worked.

3 Thread the straw needle with cotton thread; using a double thread, apply the beads, working from the first strawberry. Sew all the beaded areas of the design following the colored beading chart. The beads will lie in the opposite direction to the tent stitch background.

4 Thread the larger tapestry needle with a short length of gold thread, about 14in (36cm) long; a longer length will fray. Work the lattice framework following the chart. The lattice pattern is worked in tent stitch in gold thread over two close threads of canvas.

5 Thread the tapestry needle with three strands of crewel wool and work the background in tent stitch over two close threads.

6 To finish the glasses case, see page 121.

Single strawberry motif on the back of the Beaded Strawberry Glasses Case.

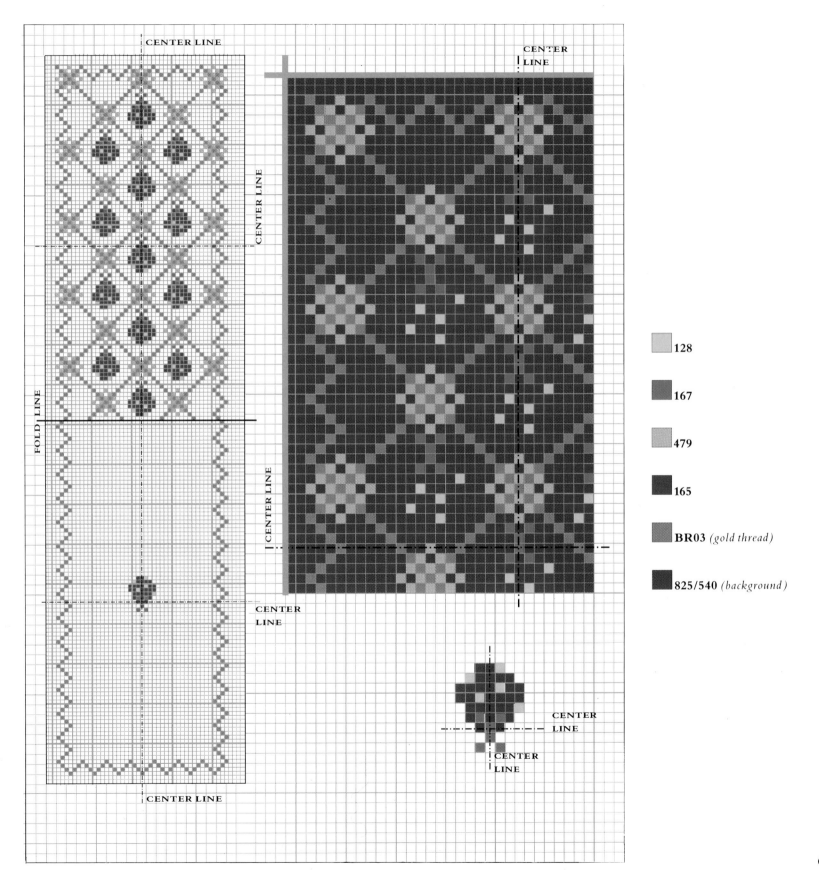

128

167

479

165

BR03 *(gold thread)*

825/540 *(background)*

BEADED FLOWER BASKET NEEDLECASE

This delightful needlecase is quick to work and would make the perfect gift for a needleworker. The beads are applied with a diagonal stitch over two close threads of canvas. The background is tent stitch using three strands of yarn over two close threads of canvas. (For stitch instructions, see page 124.) Each square on the chart represents one bead or one tent stitch.

SIZE 7½ × 4½in (19 × 11cm)

MATERIALS 12 × 9in (30 × 23cm) double-thread antique canvas, 14 holes to the inch (56 holes/10cm)
Size 9 straw needle for beading
Size 20 tapestry needle
Cotton sewing thread for applying beads

CREWEL WOOL

Appleton, use 3 strands throughout
Paternayan, use 2 strands throughout

	Appleton	Paternayan	
Background			
Peacock	647	660	I hank

Quantities are for the project using Appleton yarns

Mill Hill Glass Seed Beads

Bronze	221	I pack
Old Gold	557	I pack
Christmas Green	167	I pack
Royal Blue	020	I pack
Iris	252	I pack
Red	968	I pack
Dusty Rose	2005	I pack
Yellow	128	I pack

The delightful Beaded Flower Basket Needlecase would make an attractive addition to any workbasket.

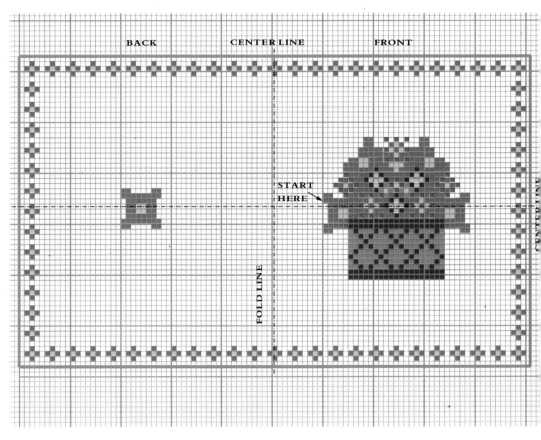

BACK   CENTER LINE   FRONT

START HERE

FOLD LINE

METHOD

1 Find the center of the canvas by folding in half in both directions and marking the horizontal and vertical lines with a basting thread.

2 Find the center point of the canvas and count to the starting point marked on the chart for the first bead to be worked.

3 Thread the straw needle with cotton and, using a double thread, apply the beads, following the colored beading chart. Complete all the beaded parts of the design, the motif on the back, and the border. The beads will lie in the opposite direction to the tent stitch background.

4 Thread the larger tapestry needle with three strands of yarn and fill in the background in tent stitch.

5 To finish the needlecase, see page 120.

■ 221
■ 557
■ 167
■ 020
□ 252
■ 968
■ 2005
□ 128
□ 647/660 *(background)*

Chapter Four

Patterns from Around the World

*M*OST *needleworkers today enjoy working on a throw pillow. Apart from the pleasure derived from stitching, the end result is a lovely decorative item, and it makes a small useful project which has every possibility of being finished.*

These designs were inspired by traditional needlework patterns, some geometric, and some floral. An intricate floral design using a lot of color is easier to work in one simple stitch – there is sufficient visual interest in the different colors. On the other hand, a geometric pattern lends itself to the use of a variety of stitches to give an interesting texture to the finished embroidery. These fascinating stitches can be used to vary the backgrounds of other designs. Planning how best to use these stitches can be very absorbing. Because many are worked over more than one thread of canvas, the work will grow quickly.

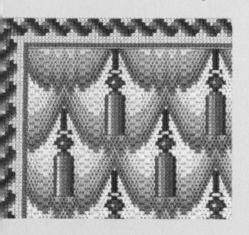

*T*ARTAN AND *S*TRAWBERRIES *P*ILLOW

The patterns of the Scottish tartans were much loved by the Victorians and often used in their embroideries. Many of the embroideries were exact replicas of tartans, with skillful interpretation of the complex details of the patterns. The strawberry motif has been used here to complement the tartans.

This design has been worked in two colors to illustrate the difference between strong vivid color combinations and soft hazy ones. It uses eight textured stitches: tent, brick, cross, checked mosaic, diagonal leaf, Hungarian variation, straight gobelin, and slanting gobelin, all of which are worked with three strands of yarn. Because a variety of stitches are used in this design, it is recommended for intermediate or advanced needleworkers. (For stitch instruc-

Tartan and Strawberries Pillow worked in a blue color scheme.

tions, see pages 122–124.) Each line on the chart represents one thread of canvas.

SIZE 16 × 16in (41 × 41cm)

MATERIALS 20 × 20in (51 × 51cm) mono de luxe antique or white (for paler colors) canvas, 14 holes to the inch (56 holes/10cm) Size 20 tapestry needle

CREWEL WOOL
Appleton, use 3 strands throughout
Paternayan, use 2 strands throughout

	Appleton	Paternayan	
Red Colors (shown on p.75 and chart)			
Scarlet	504	950	1 ¼ hanks
Rose Pink	758	901	¼ hank
Coral	863	862	¼ hank
Brown Olive (incl. background)	312	752	2 ¼ hanks
Grass Green	254	692	¾ hank
Purple	106	310	½ hank
White	992	263	¾ hank
Blue Colors (shown on left)			
Bright China Blue	743	561	1 ¼ hanks
Bright China Blue	746	560	¼ hank
Bright China Blue	741	564	¼ hank
Chocolate (incl. background)	181	475	2 ¼ hanks
Chocolate	182	463	¾ hank
Elephant	976	461	½ hank
White	992	263	¾ hank

Quantities are for the project using Appleton yarns

METHOD

1 Find the center of the canvas by folding in half in both directions and marking the horizontal and vertical lines with a basting thread.

2 Following the color code, start from the center using three strands of yarn for each stitch.

3 Work cross stitch and diagonal leaf stitch pattern in the center. Work strawberries in checked mosaic stitch.

4 Fill in the background with tent stitch, and complete with a row of cross stitch and slanting gobelin.

5 Continue to work each border pattern from the center line, following the color code and the stitch chart. Complete each border before starting the next.

6 To finish the pillow, see page 119.

START HERE →

CENTER LINE

CENTER LINE

| | 504/950 (743/561) | | 863/862 (741/564) | | 254/692 (182/463) | | 992/263 (992/263) |
| | 758/901 (746/560) | | 312/752 (181/475) | | 106/310 (976/461) | | 312/752 (181/475) *(background)* |

ENGLISH FLOWER GARDEN PILLOW

Inspired by a tapestry design from the early part of this century, this pattern is cleverly arranged so that the flowers repeat both diagonally and horizontally across the canvas. The design is appropriate for many shapes and sizes, from a small footstool to a large chair cover. It could also be made into a rug, finished with a simple border repeating the colors in the flowers of the central pattern.

This design is worked on canvas that is 12 holes to the inch (46 holes/10cm). Other counts, such as a fine small mesh or a large rug canvas could be used, although this would alter the quantities of yarn required. This interesting pattern gives plenty of scope for experimenting with color as well as size. A paler shade of background yarn would give a softer, more delicate look, while a clearer, stronger background color would give a more vivid and dramatic image.

This design uses tent stitch for the main design area, but gobelin stitch could be used for the border pattern (see pages 123–124 for stitch instructions). Each square on the chart represents one stitch.

SIZE 16½ × 16½in (42 × 42cm)

MATERIALS 21 × 21in (53 × 53cm) white mono de luxe canvas, 12 holes to the inch (46 holes/10cm), or 4in (10cm) larger than the finished design
Size 18 tapestry needle

TAPESTRY WOOL
Appleton, use 1 strand throughout
Paternayan, use 2 strands throughout

	Appleton	Paternayan	
Rose Pink	756	932	1 skein
Rose Pink	754	913	1 skein
Rose Pink	753	945	1 skein
Rose Pink	752	945	¼ hank
Early English Green	545	691	½ hank
Early English Green	544	692	½ hank
Early English Green	542	653	¼ hank
Bright China Blue	747	500	1 skein
Bright China Blue	745	560	1 skein

OPPOSITE The English Flower Garden Pillow uses a palette of many colors to achieve its country-garden atmosphere.

78

(continued overleaf)

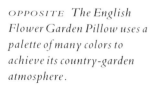

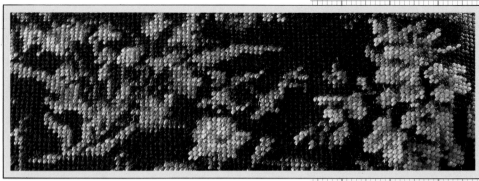

	Appleton	Paternayan	
Bright China Blue	742	562	1 skein
Cornflower	461	564	1 skein
Red Fawn	305	400	1 skein
Coral	863	862	1 skein
Autumn Yellow	474	725	¼ hank
Autumn Yellow	472	703	1 skein
Lemon	996	673	1 skein
Wine Red	713	912	1 skein
Wine Red	711	914	1 skein
Bright Peacock	833	661	1 skein
Bright Peacock	832	662	¼ hank
Bright Peacock	831	662	1 skein
Purple	104	312	1 skein
Purple	101	313	1 skein
Pastel Mauve	884	314	1 skein
Cornflower	464	542	1 skein
Cornflower	463	543	1 skein
Cornflower	462	544	1 skein
Brown Olive	313	751	1 skein
Olive Green	244	641	1 skein
Grass Green	253	693	1 skein
Drab Green	331	644	1 skein
Pastel Yellow	872	715	1 hank
Background			
Wine Red	716	912	4 hanks

Quantities are for the project using Appleton yarns

METHOD

1 Find the center of the canvas by folding it in half in both directions and marking the horizontal and vertical lines with a basting thread.

2 Using one strand of tapestry wool, start from the center and work the first motif in tent stitch, following the stitch chart and the color code. Continue working the pattern and filling in the background as work progresses to the edge of the border.

3 Work the border in gobelin stitch over two threads of canvas.

4 To finish the pillow, see instructions page 119.

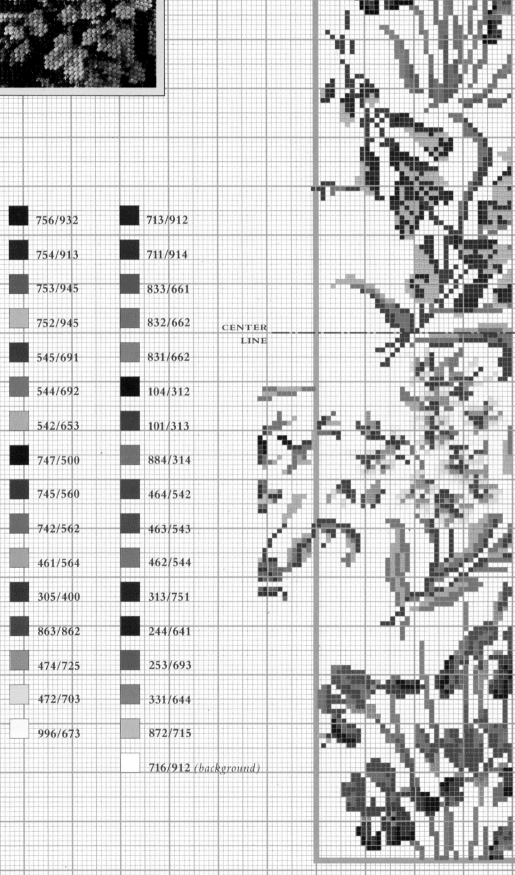

Color key:

- 756/932
- 754/913
- 753/945
- 752/945
- 545/691
- 544/692
- 542/653
- 747/500
- 745/560
- 742/562
- 461/564
- 305/400
- 863/862
- 474/725
- 472/703
- 996/673
- 713/912
- 711/914
- 833/661
- 832/662
- 831/662
- 104/312
- 101/313
- 884/314
- 464/542
- 463/543
- 462/544
- 313/751
- 244/641
- 253/693
- 331/644
- 872/715
- 716/912 *(background)*

CENTER LINE

CENTER LINE

Bokhara Pillow

Rich and colorful embroideries came from Turkey, Greece, and Persia where intricate designs were created on costumes and household items.

This warm strong pattern incorporates textured stitches to give an interesting finish. The design uses four decorative stitches: tent, cross, straight gobelin, and slanting gobelin. Because of the number of different stitches used, this design is recommended for intermediate or advanced needleworkers. (For stitch instructions see pages 122–124.) Each line on the chart represents one thread of canvas.

SIZE 16 × 15½in (41 × 39cm)

MATERIALS 19½ × 19½in (50 × 50cm) mono de luxe antique canvas, 14 holes to the inch (56 holes/10cm)
Size 20 tapestry needle

CREWEL WOOL

Appleton, use 3 strands throughout
Paternayan, use 2 strands throughout

	Appleton	Paternayan	
Bright Terracotta	224	931	1 hank
Bright Terracotta	226	930	½ hank
Grass Green	254	692	½ hank
Brown Olive	311	751	½ hank
Brown Grounding	586	421	1 skein
Bright China Blue	747	500	2½ hanks
Bright Peacock	833	661	½ hank

Quantities are for the project using Appleton yarns

METHOD

1 Find the center of the canvas by folding in half in both directions and marking the horizontal and vertical lines with a basting thread.

2 Use three strands of yarn throughout. Count from the chart and use colors according to color code to work the stitches.

3 Counting the threads of canvas from the center point, work the inner border.

4 Work each diagonal band starting from the corner of the cross stitch inner border. Fill in the background with tent stitch as work progresses. To finish, complete the border.

5 To finish the pillow, see instructions page 119.

OPPOSITE The lively combination of pattern and color in the Bokhara Pillow produces a warm Mediterranean feel, and the textured stitches give an interesting finish.

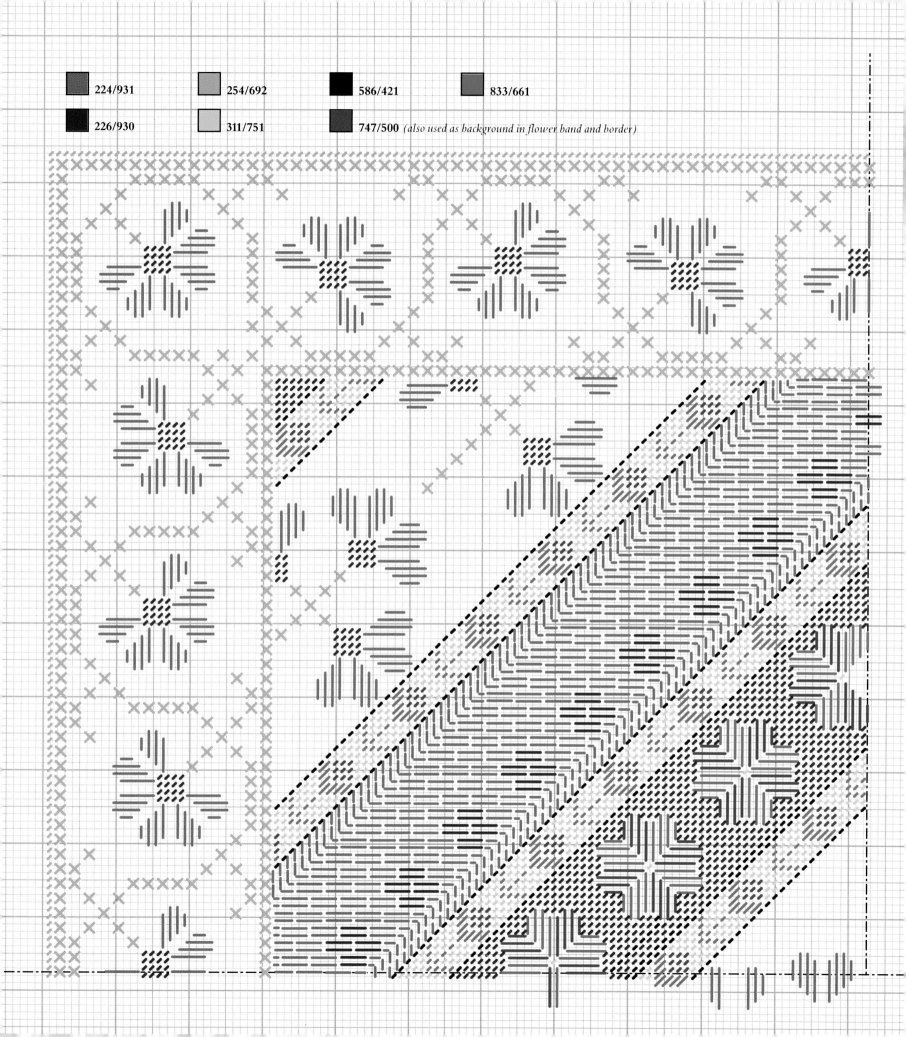

224/931   254/692   586/421   833/661

226/930   311/751   747/500 *(also used as background in flower band and border)*

CENTER LINE

START HERE

THIS CHART REPRESENTS HALF THE DESIGN

CENTER LINE

Florentine Tassels Pillow

The popular bargello pattern used in this design is easy and quick to work, because the stitches are sewn over several threads of canvas at a time. The tassel motif (popular in Victorian border designs) creates an interesting project and prevents the needlework from becoming repetitive. The whole design is finished off with a twisting rope border to match the tassels.

Although the design is shown here in a pale-green background with stronger colors for the tassels, another pastel background with harmonizing colors would be just as effective. A gray background with white and black tassels would look stunning.

This design uses three decorative textured stitches: Florentine, cross, and tent stitch; all the stitches use three strands of yarn. Because the pillow is quick and easy to make, it is well suited for a beginner. (For stitch instructions see pages 122–124.) Each line on the chart represents one thread of canvas.

SIZE 13 × 14in (33 × 36cm)

MATERIALS 19 × 19in (48 × 48cm) mono de luxe antique canvas, 14 holes to the inch (56 holes/10cm)
Size 20 tapestry needle

CREWEL WOOL

Appleton, use 3 strands throughout
Paternayan, use 2 strands throughout

	Appleton	Paternayan	
Background Colors			
Pastel	873	615	½ hank
Pastel	874†	624	1¼ hanks
Gray Green	352	605	½ hank
Gray Green	353*	604	½ hank
Gray Green	354	603	¼ hank
Gray Green	355*	603	½ hank
Blue Tassels			
Pastel	875	236	1 skein
Dull Marine Blue	321*	513	¼ hank
Dull Marine Blue	322	513	1 skein
Dull Marine Blue	324*	512	¼ hank
Dull Marine Blue	325*	511	¼ hank

OPPOSITE The traditional Victorian tassel design is set against a subtle background of Florentine stitch.

(continued overleaf)

Pink Tassels

Bright Terracotta	221	490	I skein
Bright Terracotta	222*	933	¼ hank
Bright Terracotta	223	923	I skein
Bright Terracotta	224*	931	¼ hank
Bright Terracotta	226*	930	¼ hank

Quantities are for the project using Appleton yarns

* colors also used in rope border pattern   † border background color

METHOD

1 Find the center of the canvas by folding in half in both directions and marking the horizontal and vertical lines with a basting thread.

2 Using three strands of yarn throughout, start from the center with the first cross stitch.

3 Complete the first tassel and fill in the background around the first motif in Florentine stitch.

4 Work the bargello pattern to the next tassel motif. Continue working the motifs and the background from the chart until the center pattern is completed.

5 Work one row of tent and then one row of cross stitch around the central design before starting the outer border. Counting from the first row of cross stitch, start the rope border from the center line in cross stitch. Complete the background by filling it in with cross stitch.

6 Finish with a row of cross stitch and then a row of tent stitch.

7 To finish the pillow, see page 119.

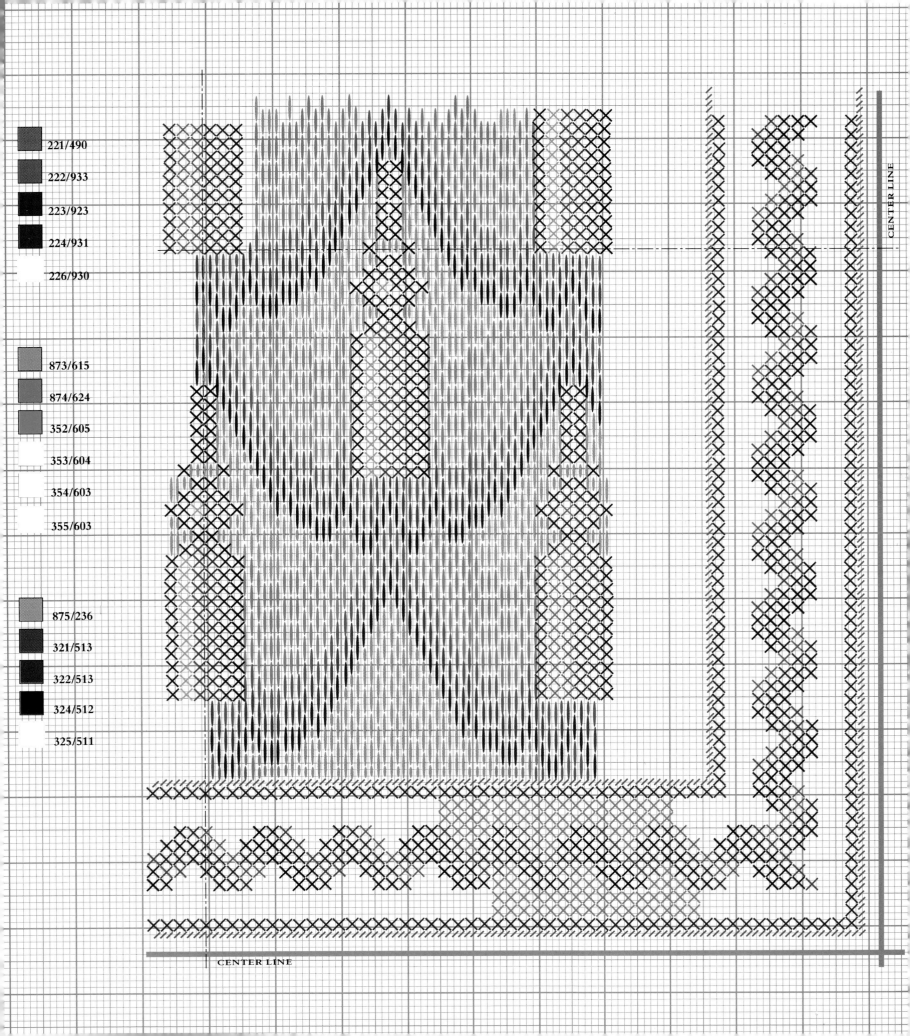

221/490
222/933
223/923
224/931
226/930

873/615
874/624
352/605
353/604
354/603
355/603

875/236
321/513
322/513
324/512
325/511

CENTER LINE

CENTER LINE

CENTER LINE

Chapter Five

BORDER PATTERNS

*M*OST *needlepoint is improved by the addition of a border. A border frames and balances the work and gives the design an individual touch. Experiment with different colors and border patterns on a spare piece of canvas. Scale can be very important, as some patterns can take a wide border and others are better with a simple narrow one. Many borders are worked in tent stitch and reflect the pattern or motif used in the central design; others are worked in a combination of different stitches and repeated sequences.*

There are differing degrees of complexity when it comes to borders. The easiest ones use straight stitches, like the gobelin border used on the Queen Mary's Tree Pillow (page 15). Try using two colors, working one row in one color and the next in another. There is no need to count these borders onto the finished design; they will always fit.

Borders using wider stitches worked over two or more threads of the canvas are a bit more difficult. The number of threads along each side of the design must be counted to see whether the chosen stitch combination will fit. The border must go around the design and meet in the corners. Sometimes extra rows must be worked to the main pattern so that the border will fit.

A simple way to create a border without counting is to baste a diagonal line from the center of the design to the corner of the planned finish line. The stitches are then worked to this diagonal line and started again along the next edge of the design, giving a neat mitered effect.

The most difficult borders are repeating intertwined ones, which are traditionally used on samplers. The mitered corners need to fall in exactly the right place to contain the central design, so the pattern must be drawn on graph paper first, counting each line of the graph paper as a thread of canvas. The center of the border is then positioned to fit the center of the finished edge of the design.

There are two easy ways to figure out mitered corners. The first method requires a small mirror. Draw the design on graph paper; then place the small mirror diagonally across the border at the most suitable place for turning so that the design is reflected at a right angle. Use the mirror image as a guide for the next part of the pattern. The second method is to make a tracing from the wrong side of the original. Put the two together at a right angle. Then make a final tracing of the miter and draw it on the graph paper.

The border patterns featured in this chapter have been divided into three groups: simple borders worked in yellows and blues; slightly more complicated borders, worked in corals and greens; more difficult intertwining patterns, worked in greens and pinks. Finally, there are two pretty flower borders worked in tent stitch; both are simple to work, but they need to be counted onto the canvas to make sure the mitered corners fit. These borders can be mixed with others to create designs like the one used for the cover of the Gentleman's Gout Stool (page 110). They would also make attractive border patterns for a throw-pillow cover.

Let this small collection of border designs encourage you to experiment. Design and work your own combinations of different stitches to bring a personal touch to your canvas embroidery.

One strand of tapestry yarn has been used to work all the borders. For each border follow the chart, counting the stitches onto the canvas. For stitch instructions, see pages 122–124.

Yellow and Blue Borders

These borders use straight gobelin or cushion stitch. Patterns six and ten can be worked directly onto the canvas without counting. All the rest have mitered corners; for these, draw a line from the corner of the central design to the corner edge of the area of canvas to be worked. Then work the pattern as far as this diagonal line. Restart and reverse the pattern to match the first side. (For stitch instructions see pages 122 and 123.) Each line on the chart represents one thread of canvas.

PATTERN ONE Use four colors; stitch in straight gobelin.

PATTERN TWO Use three colors; stitch in straight gobelin.

PATTERN THREE Use three colors; stitch in straight gobelin over four threads of canvas throughout.

PATTERN FOUR Use four colors; stitch in straight gobelin.

PATTERN FIVE Use two colors; stitch in straight gobelin.

PATTERN SIX Use two colors; stitch in straight gobelin over two threads of canvas throughout.

PATTERN SEVEN Use two colors; stitch in straight gobelin.

PATTERN EIGHT Use six colors; stitch in cushion stitch.

PATTERN NINE Use two colors; stitch in straight gobelin.

PATTERN TEN Use two colors; stitch in straight gobelin and cushion stitch.

RIGHT These very simple borders use straight gobelin or cushion stitch.

841/704

472/703

474/725

742/562

745/560

747/500

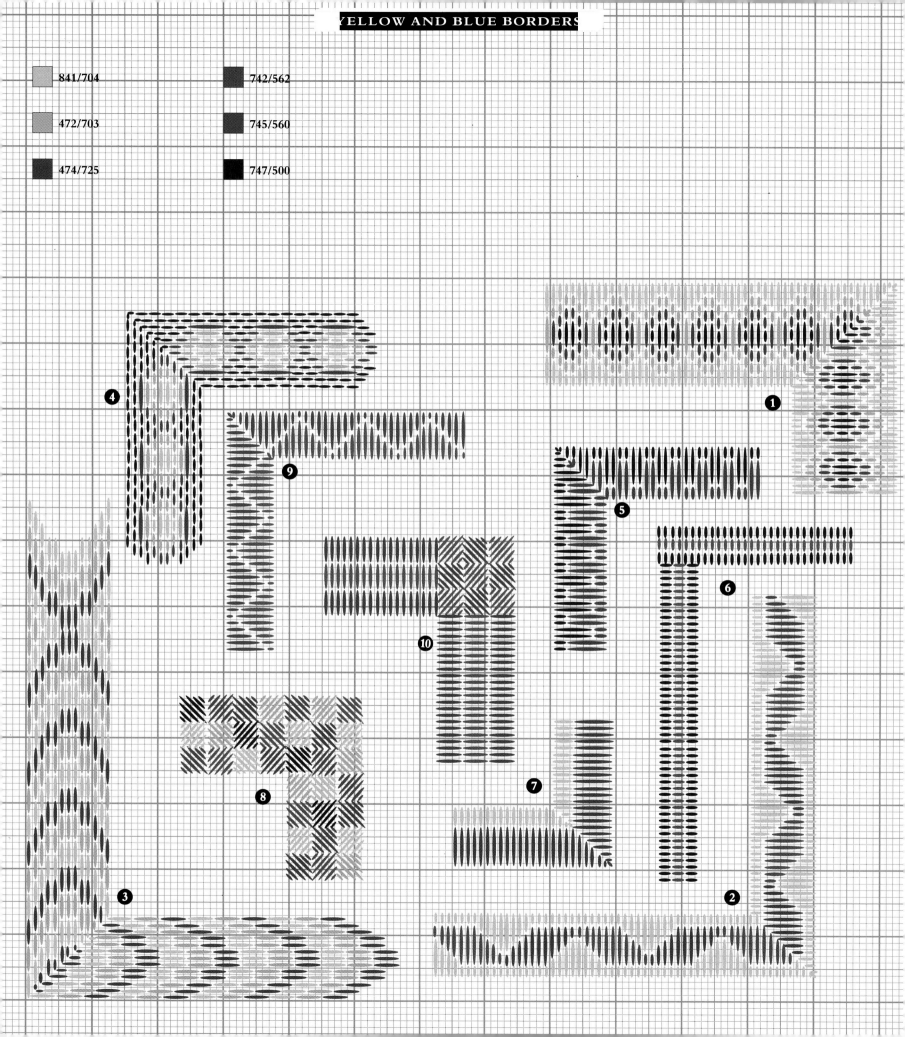

881/262   251/653   255/651   861/855   863/862   726/860

PROJECT TWO

Coral and Green Borders

The patterns for these borders are fairly easy to work. Most of the stitches used are straight, and because they are worked over a varying number of threads of canvas, there is an interesting selection of borders to choose from. These designs must be counted and centered on the canvas so that the mitered corners fall at the correct position of the repeat. (For stitch instructions, see pages 122–123.) Each line on the chart represents one thread of canvas.

PATTERN ONE Use two colors; stitch in straight gobelin.

PATTERN TWO Use three colors; stitch in straight gobelin.

PATTERN THREE Use three colors; stitch in straight gobelin.

PATTERN FOUR Use two colors; stitch in cushion stitch.

PATTERN FIVE Use three colors; stitch in straight gobelin.

PATTERN SIX Use three colors; stitch in straight gobelin.

PATTERN SEVEN Use two colors; stitch in straight gobelin.

These fairly easy borders use mostly straight stitches.

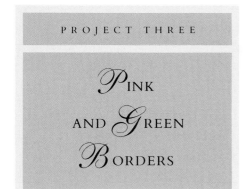

These floral patterns are useful for finishing a sampler. They are a little more difficult to work as they are repeating patterns, but they become easier as work progresses. All these borders need to be worked out on graph paper to center them on the canvas and position the mitered corners. The miters do not have to be identical to those shown here. (See page 123 for guidance on mitering corners.) The backgrounds should be finished in tent stitch (not shown here. For stitch instructions see pages 122–124). Each line on the chart represents one thread of canvas.

PATTERN ONE Use four colors. First, work a portion of the curving cross stitches and work the flowers in straight gobelin. Then fill in the centers of the flowers with single cross stitches. Work the background in tent stitch as the pattern progresses.

PATTERN TWO Use four colors. First, work the straight gobelin stitches, leaving spaces for the cross stitches to twine in and out of the line. Then work the cross stitches. Last, fill in with arrowhead stitch. Work the background in tent stitch as the pattern progresses. Work each section of border before moving on to the next section.

PATTERN THREE Use three colors. First, work a portion of the curving cross stitch, then the leaf and sloping gobelin stitches. Next, work the strawberries in brick stitch. Fill in the background with tent stitch.

PATTERN FOUR Use three colors. First, work a length of the curving cross stitch. Then work the cross stitch beneath the flowers. Fill in each section with a flower in cushion stitch. Fill in the background in tent stitch as the pattern progresses.

PATTERN FIVE Use four colors. First, work a portion of the curving tent stitch. Then work the diagonal leaf stitch. Fill in the background in tent stitch as the pattern progresses.

These more intricate floral borders use textured stitches in repeating patterns.

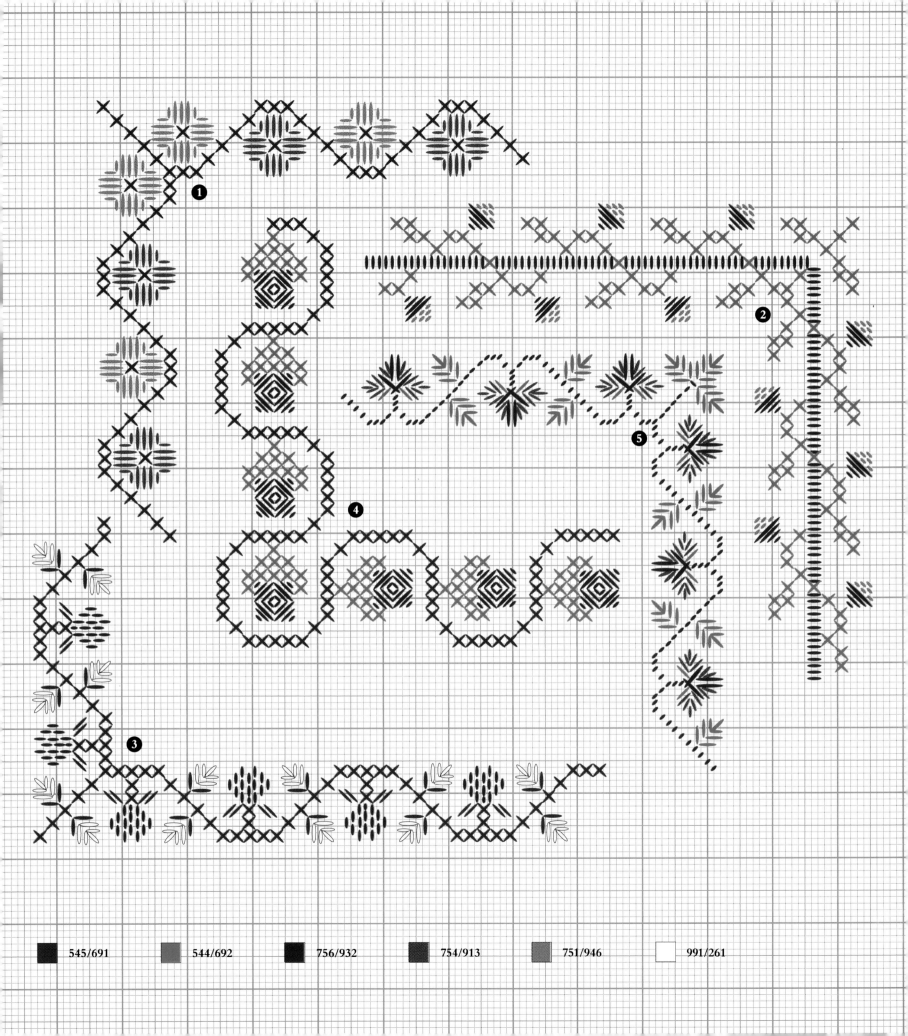

545/691   544/692   756/932   754/913   751/946   991/261

Rose Border

This border of pink rosebuds and roses set among leaves creates a traditional pattern for a pillow square or sampler. The pattern has been reversed in the middle of each section so that the corners link up well. This border could be extended by repeating the pattern, or it could be reduced by omitting a small section. This pattern, which is worked in tent stitch, could also be worked in bands across the canvas for a pillow cover or square footstool, or one band could be worked to make a bell pull. (For stitch instructions, see page 124.) Each square on the chart represents one stitch on the canvas.

SIZE 19 × 18in (48 × 46cm)

MATERIALS Mono de luxe antique canvas, 12 holes to the inch (46 holes/10cm)
Size 18 tapestry needle

TAPESTRY WOOL

Appleton, use 1 strand throughout
Paternayan, use 2 strands throughout

	Appleton	Paternayan	
Rose Pink	755	932	½ hank
Rose Pink	754	913	½ hank
Rose Pink	751	946	½ hank
Bright Yellow	551	773	¼ hank
Early English Green	545	691	½ hank
Early English Green	543	693	½ hank

Quantities are for the project using Appleton yarns

METHOD

1 Following the color code and the stitch chart, work in tent stitch, starting from the center line. Fill in the background as work progresses.

OPPOSITE The pretty Rose Border could frame a traditional pillow or sampler.

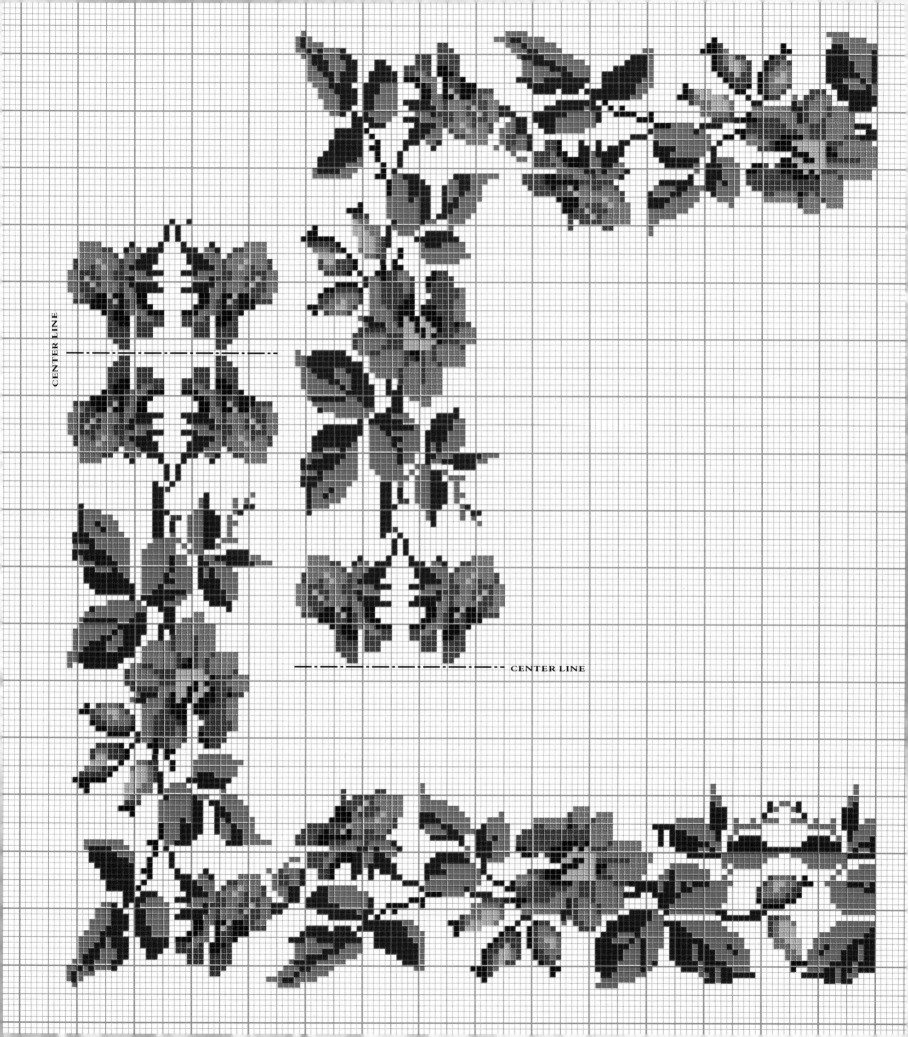

CENTER LINE

CENTER LINE

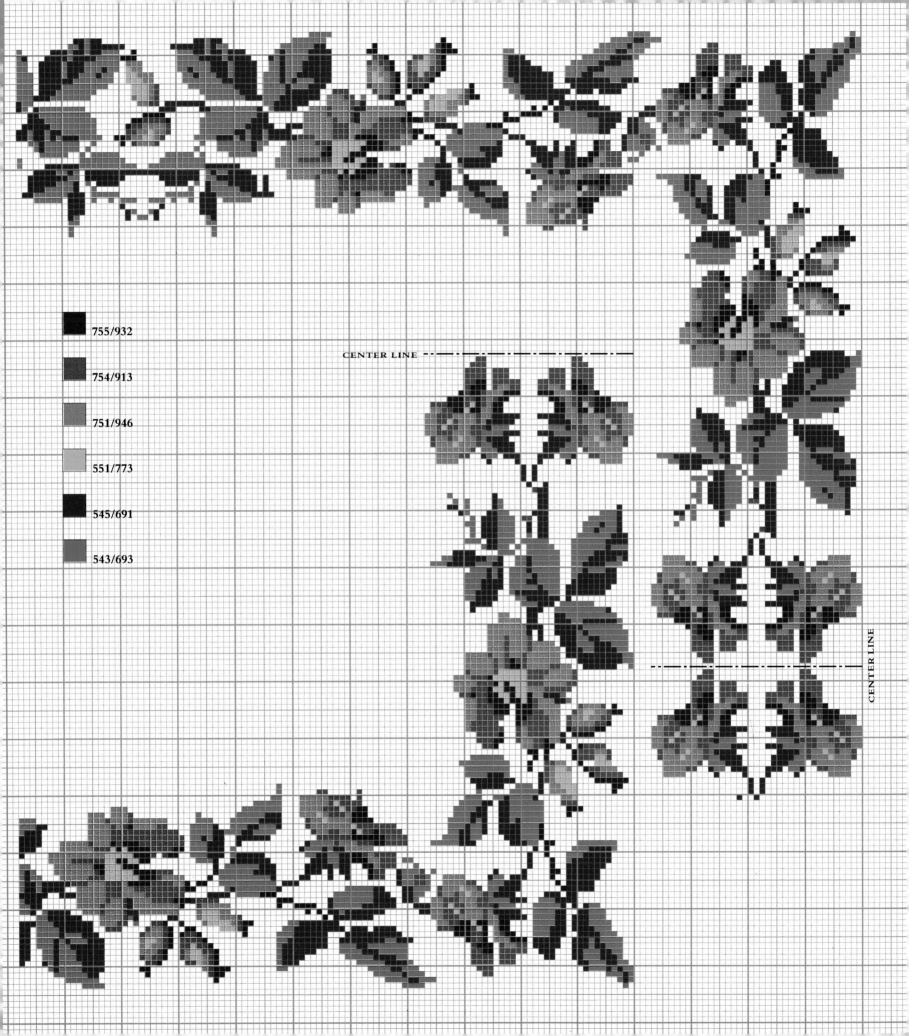

CENTER LINE

CENTER LINE

755/932

754/913

751/946

551/773

545/691

543/693

Pansy and Ribbon Border and Gentleman's Gout Stool

The delicate coloring used to work this border has produced a soft attractive design of cornflowers, pansies, and leaves tied with a ribbon. It has been made to form a frame, with the pattern reversed in the center at the top and bottom so that the bows work correctly at each corner. The photograph on page 110 shows this design worked in bands with a barley-twist pattern between each band. The Gentleman's Gout Stool is a good example of how border patterns can be developed into complete projects. This pattern can be extended in length and width to fit any shape (for example, a bell pull).

Other color combinations could be used to produce a much stronger pattern. The design is worked in tent stitch. (For stitch instructions, see page 124.) Each square on the chart represents one stitch on the canvas.

PATTERN REPEAT Every 60 threads

MATERIALS Mono de luxe antique canvas, 12 holes to the inch (46 holes/10cm) Size 18 tapestry needle

TAPESTRY WOOL

Appleton, use 1 strand throughout
Paternayan, use 2 strands throughout
The following quantities are for one pattern repeat

	Appleton	Paternayan	
Heraldic Gold	841	704	½ hank
Heraldic Gold	842	734	¼ hank
Heraldic Gold	843	733	¼ hank
Early English Green	543	693	1 skein
Early English Green	546	691	1 skein
Purple	102	313	1 skein
Purple	103	312	1 skein
Bright China Blue	742	562	1 skein
Bright China Blue	746	560	1 skein
Background			
Brown Grounding	588	420	1 hank

Quantities are for the project using Appleton yarns

METHOD

1 Following the color code and the stitch chart, work in tent stitch, start from the center line. Fill in the background as work progresses.

OPPOSITE The Pansy and Ribbon Border is a repeating pattern which makes an ideal border. It can also be used across the canvas as seen on the Gentleman's Gout Stool (page 110).

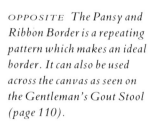

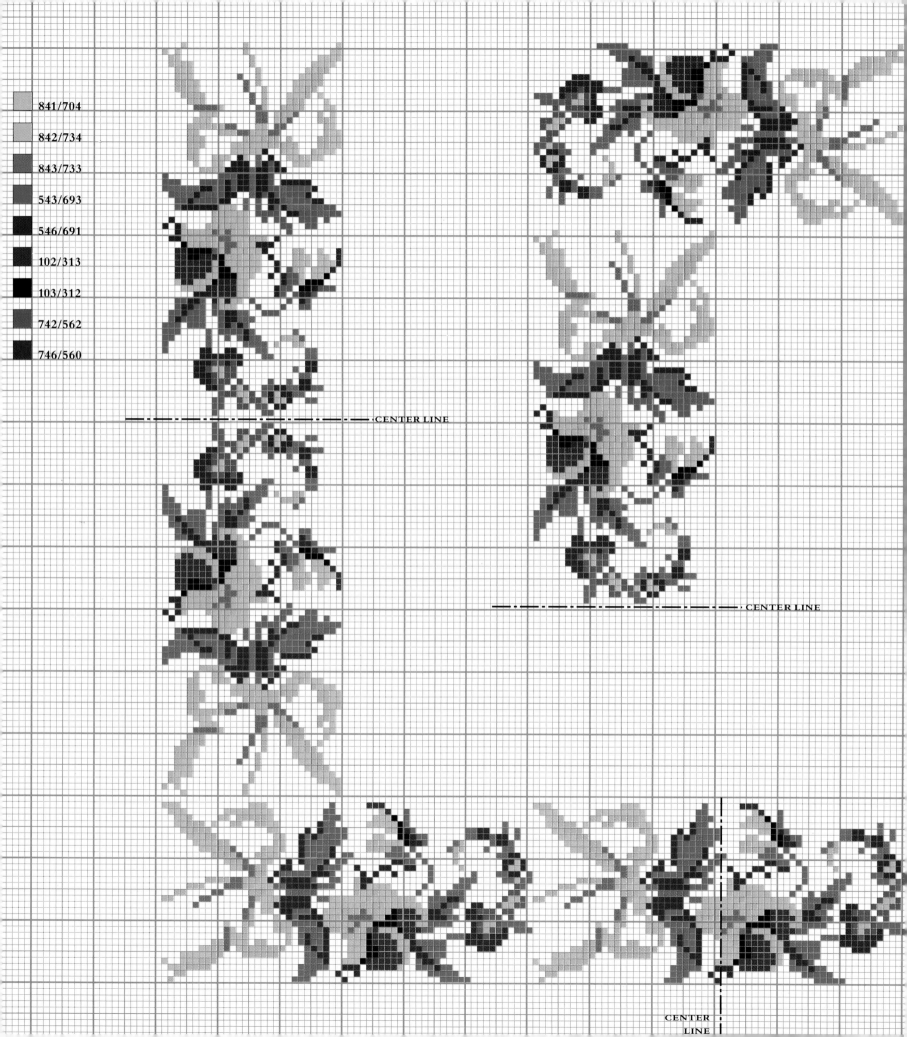

841/704

842/734

843/733

543/693

546/691

102/313

103/312

742/562

746/560

CENTER LINE

CENTER LINE

CENTER
LINE

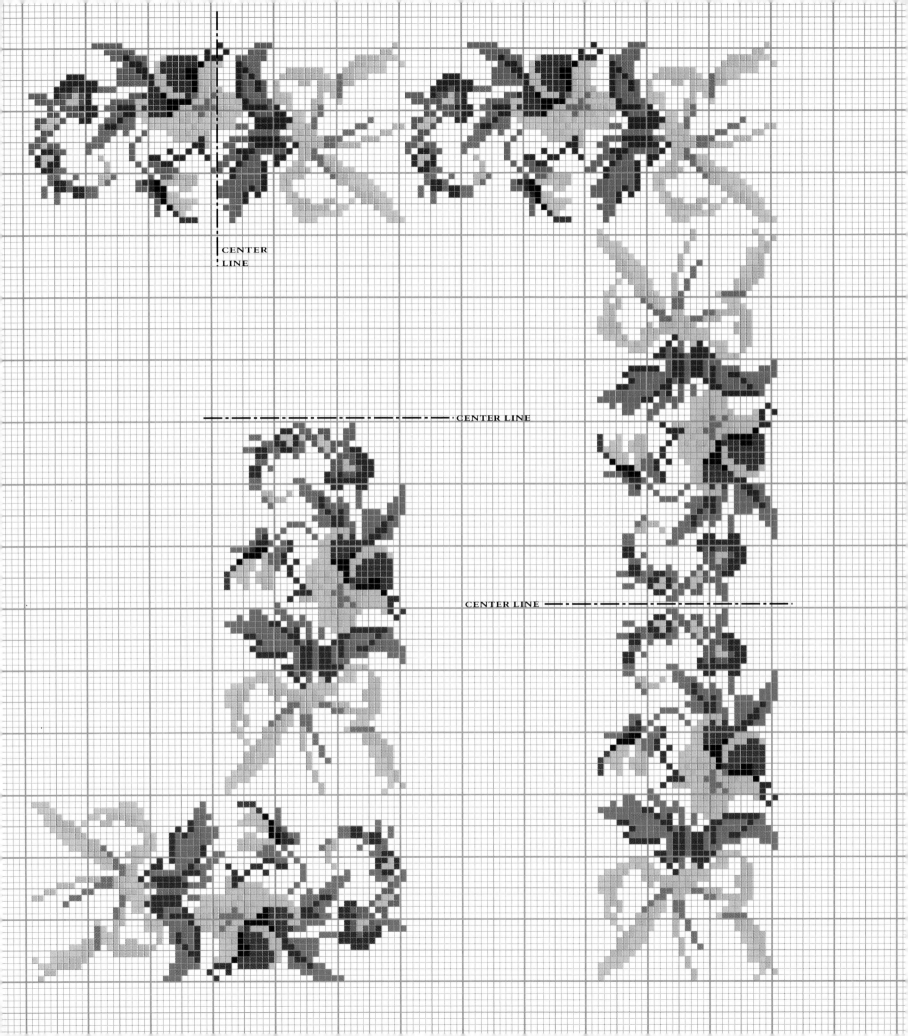

CENTER
LINE

CENTER LINE

CENTER LINE

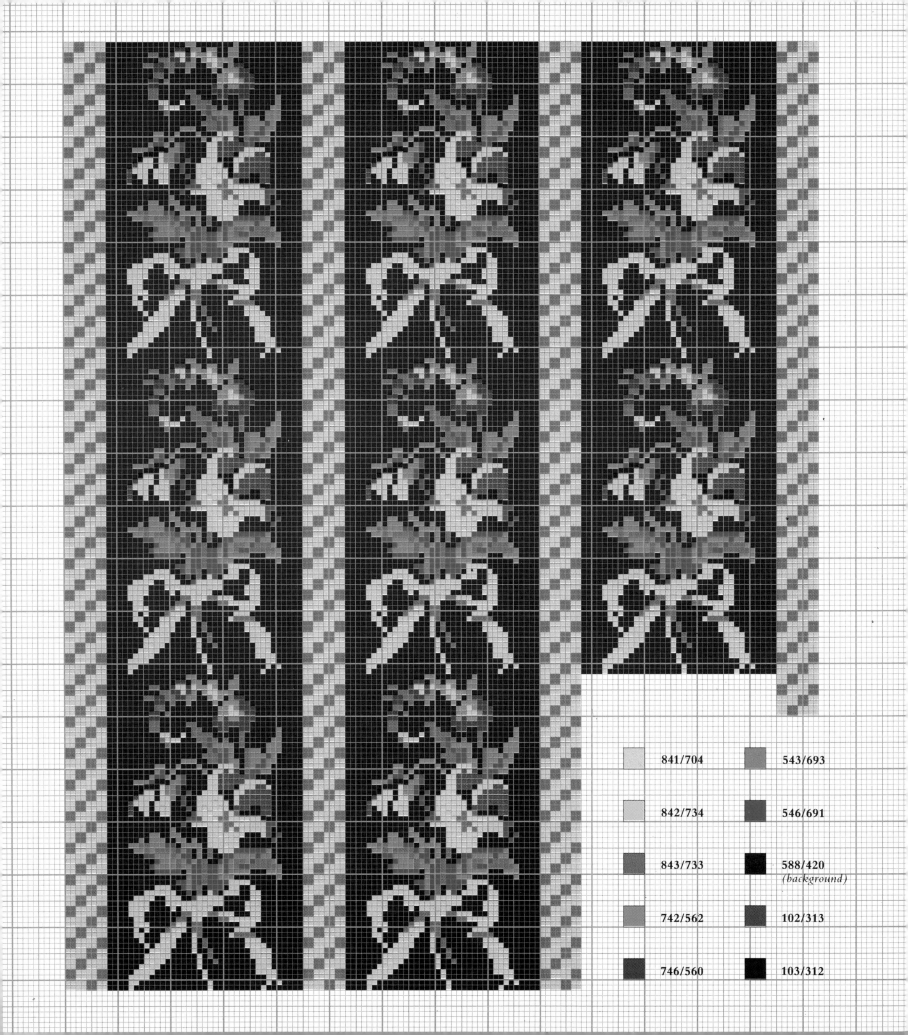

841/704
543/693

842/734
546/691

843/733
588/420
(background)

742/562
102/313

746/560
103/312

A Potpourri Of Patterns

This design brings together a variety of stitches and patterns that have been used throughout this book and illustrates how they can be used together to create a complete design.

By restricting the colors to six shades of pink, green and white, what looks like a difficult design is made relatively simple. Experiment with other patterns and stitches in this book to produce your own very personal piece of work.

Each line on the chart represents one thread of canvas.

SIZE 13¾ × 14¼in (35 × 36cm)

MATERIALS 20 × 20in (50 × 50cm) mono de luxe antique canvas, 12 holes to the inch (46 holes/10cm)
Size 18 tapestry needle

TAPESTRY WOOL

Appleton, use I strand throughout
Paternayan, use 2 strands throughout

	Appleton	Paternayan	
Early English Green	545	691	1½ hanks
Early English Green	542	653	I hank
White	992	263	½ hank
Bright Terracotta	222	933	I hank
Rose Pink	753	945	½ hank
Rose Pink	751	946	I hank

Quantities are for the project using Appleton yarns

METHOD

1 Find the center of the canvas by folding in half in both directions and marking the horizontal and vertical lines with a basting thread.

2 Following the color code, and using one strand of yarn, begin at the center. Work the first stitch pattern.

3 Complete each stitch pattern before starting on the next, referring to the stitch directory (pages 122–124), and counting the stitches from the chart onto the canvas.

The Potpourri Pillow has been created by combining different patterns.

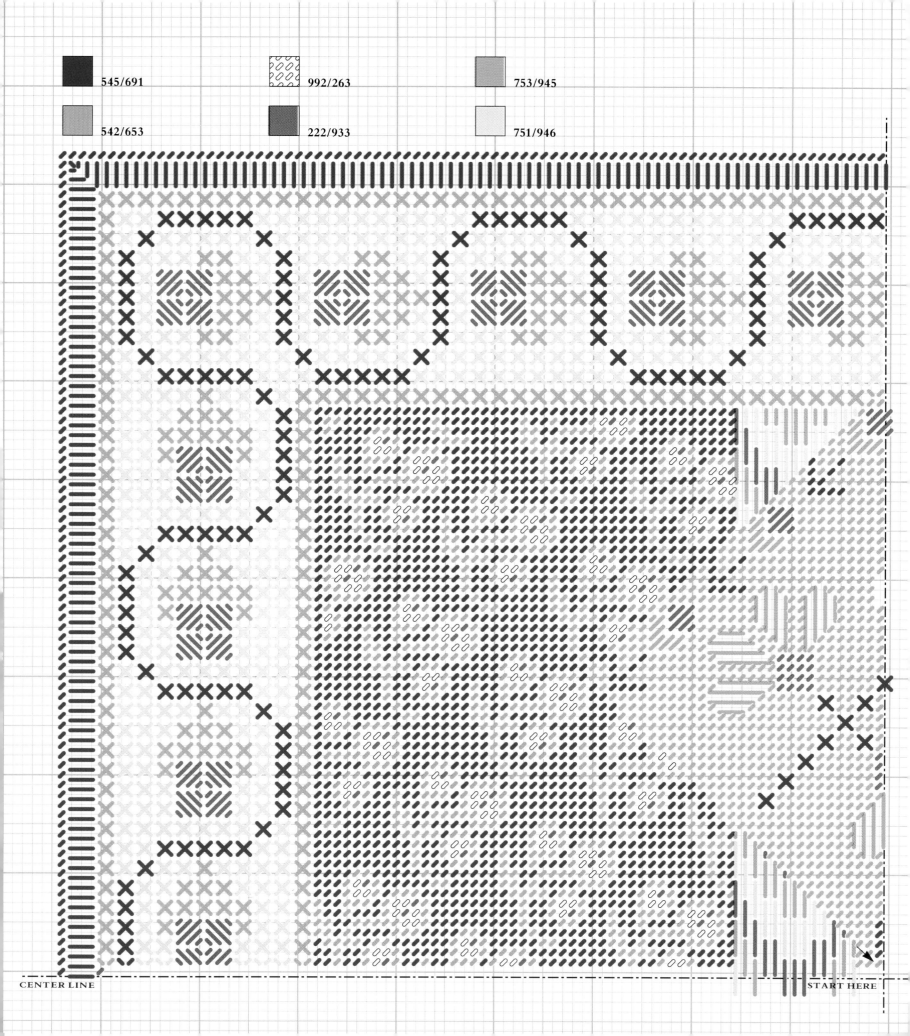

545/691

992/263

753/945

542/653

222/933

751/946

CENTER LINE

START HERE

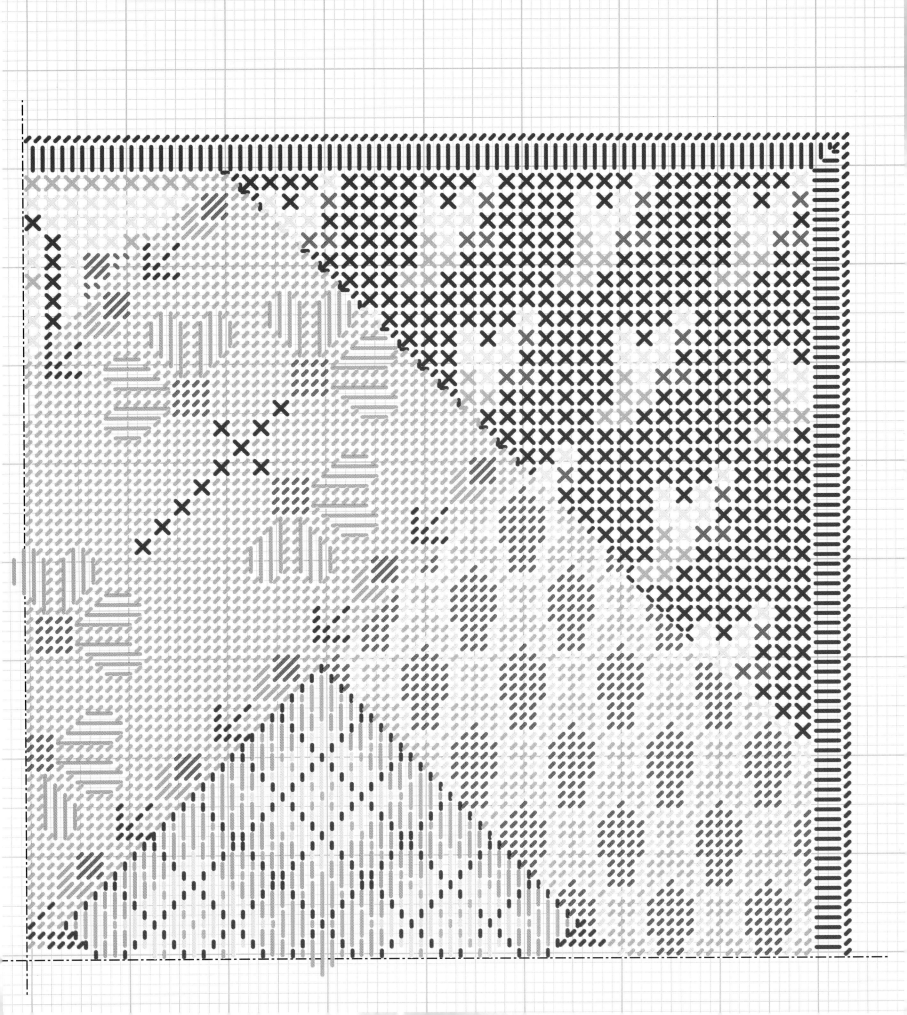

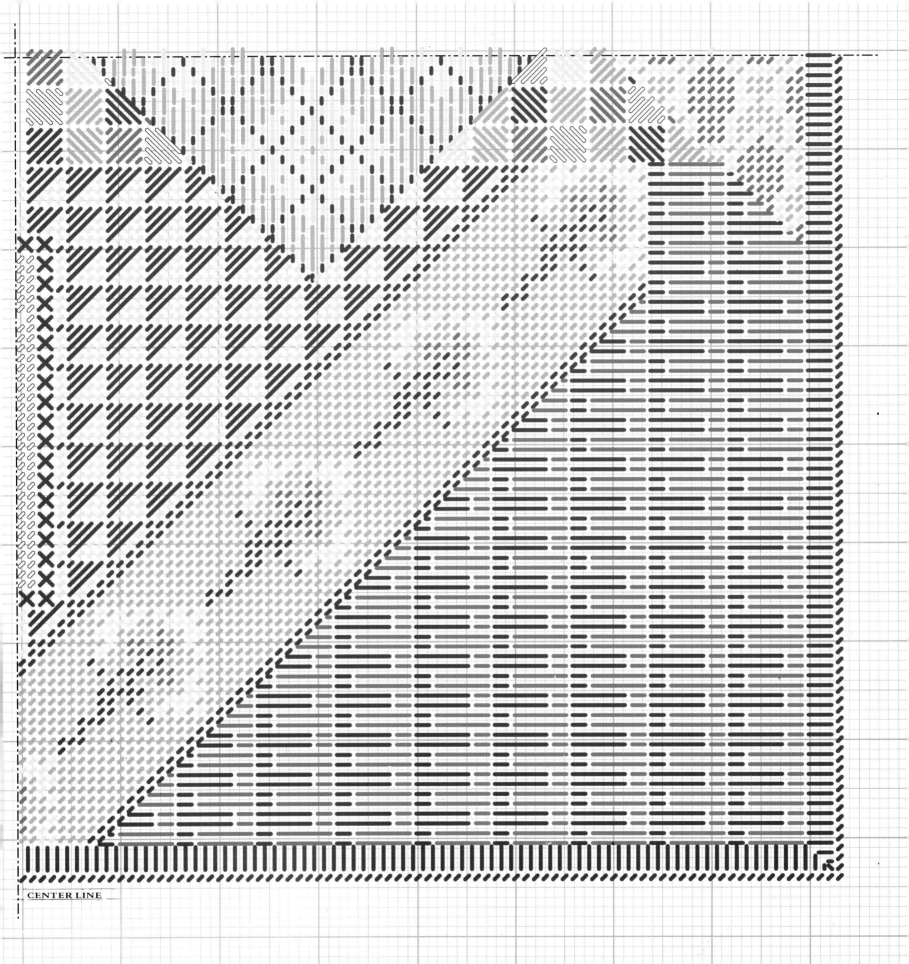

CENTER LINE

Finishing Techniques

*A*LMOST *all stitched canvases are distorted because the process of stitching, particularly when using diagonal stitches, pulls the canvas out of shape. This can be minimized by using a roller frame while you work, but most canvases will still need blocking to achieve a straight and pleasing finished result.*

Some canvases may be quite difficult to block, so I advise using a professional blocking and framing service to prevent disappointment after your many hours of work. Your local needlecraft retailer may be able to recommend or even offer such a service. I also recommend using a professional to finish the final projects like pillows and seat covers. However, if you wish to tackle your own blocking, framing, and finishing, I hope the following instructions will be useful.

BLOCKING

MATERIALS

■ Wooden board larger than the canvas and soft enough to take tacks or nails
■ Small tacks or stainless steel nails
■ Piece of blotting paper larger than the finished design (or use two pieces joined together)
■ Carpenter's square and ruler
■ Hammer and pliers
■ Pencil or waterproof marker

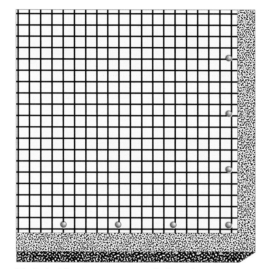

Tack the blotting paper onto the board.

1 To prepare the board, draw grid lines on the blotting paper at 1in (2.5cm) intervals; tack it to the board. Moisten the back of the canvas with a fairly wet (but not dripping) sponge and place canvas face up over the squared blotting paper, using the grid lines on the blotting paper as a guide to get the sides straight and the corners square.
2 Tack it in place, gently stretching and pulling it into shape. Place the tacks 1in (2.5cm) from the edge of the design and 1in (2.5cm) apart. Do not hammer the tacks all the way into the board because the tacks may have to be repositioned as the canvas is pulled and stretched. When the canvas is completely square, hammer

Tack the canvas onto the blotting paper.

the tacks firmly into the board. If necessary, add more tacks at ½in (12mm) to ¼in (6mm) intervals so that the canvas is completely taut, but never stretch the canvas so tightly that the threads are straining against the tacks.
3 Let the canvas dry naturally in a horizontal position away from direct heat or sunshine for as long as possible (36 to 48 hours). Badly distorted canvases may need to be blocked more than once.

If a template has been used, draw the template outline onto the blotting paper. Then follow the instructions above to block the canvas so that it fits the template perfectly. If the design is worked entirely in tent stitch, block the canvas face down on the blotting paper to even out the surface of the stitched canvas. If textured stitches have been used, block right side up so that the stitches are not flattened. Beaded designs should also be blocked right side up.

FRAMING

It is advisable to use a good professional framer, but if this is not possible, here are a few guidelines.

❚ Firm board or plastic sheet, cut to fit into the recess of your chosen frame; can be slightly larger than the worked area to give a margin of unworked canvas
❚ Strong cotton thread to lace across the board
❚ Tacks
❚ Large tapestry needle
❚ Small hammer

1 Block the canvas back into shape if necessary, following the instructions on page 118.
2 Place the canvas face down on a clean surface and center the board on the back of the canvas.
3 Thread the tapestry needle with strong cotton thread and lace the canvas onto the board from top to bottom and from side to side, pulling and holding the thread to make sure the design stays centered and straight.
4 Mount into the frame; tack into place.

PLAIN-EDGE PILLOW

❚ Backing fabric 4in (10cm) larger than the finished design
❚ Pillow form 2in (5cm) larger than the finished design
❚ Pins
❚ Zipper (optional)

1 After the canvas has been blocked, machine stitch two rows around the design ½in (12mm) from the edge of the worked area of canvas to prevent fraying. Trim to leave a 1in (2.5cm) seam allowance all around the design.
2 Cut the backing fabric to the same size as the trimmed canvas.
3 Pin or baste the fabric and canvas together with right sides facing, leaving

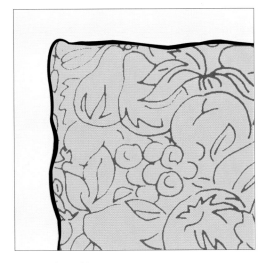

Plain-edge pillow.

an opening on one side large enough to insert the pillow form. Machine stitch the sides together as close as possible to the worked needlepoint. Trim and overcast all raw edges; trim the corners. Turn right side out through the opening.
4 Insert the pillow form and close opening with slipstitches along the seam line. If preferred, a zipper can be stitched into the opening.

DECORATIVE CORD-EDGE PILLOW

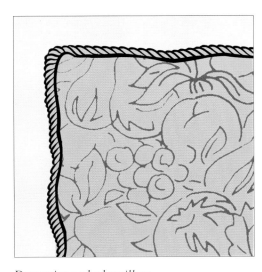

Decorative cord-edge pillow.

❚ Backing fabric 4in (10cm) larger than the finished design
❚ Pillow form 2in (5cm) larger than the finished design
❚ Decorative cord 2in (5cm) longer than the measurement around the outside edge of the finished design
❚ Pins
❚ Zipper (optional)

1 Follow the instructions for a plain-edge pillow, but leave a 1in (2.5cm) opening along one side for the ends of the cord to be tucked in.
2 Bind the ends of the cord to prevent fraying.
3 Slipstitch the cord around the edge of the pillow. Finish the ends by splicing or stitching the ends into the opening and sew it closed.

PIPED-EDGE PILLOW

❚ Backing fabric 4in (10cm) larger than the finished design plus an extra piece large enough to cut bias strips 2in (5cm) wide and the length of the outer edge of the finished, blocked design
❚ Piping 4in (10cm) longer than the measurement around the edge of the finished design
❚ Pillow form 2in (5cm) larger than the finished design
❚ Pins
❚ Zipper (optional)

1 Cut 2in (5cm) wide bias strips of fabric. Join together to make one strip the length required to cover the piping cord.
2 With wrong sides together, fold the bias strip in half, with the piping cord inside. Sew the strip together close to the cord to make piping.

119

Piped-edge pillow.

3 Baste the piping to the seam line on the right side of the pillow front. Join the ends by unraveling about ¾in (2cm) of the cord at both ends and cutting to different lengths before re-twisting to make a smooth join. Neatly hand stitch the ends of the fabric covering.

4 Complete as for plain-edge pillow.

NEEDLECASE

▪ Backing fabric 4in (10cm) larger than the finished, blocked design
▪ Braid or piping 2in (5cm) longer than the measurement around the outside edge of the finished design (optional)
▪ Felt large enough to make four to six leaves to fit inside the needlecase
▪ Length of narrow ribbon for ties
▪ Pins
▪ Pinking shears

1 Machine stitch two or three rows ½in (12mm) from the edge of the worked area of canvas to prevent fraying. Trim to leave a 1in (2.5cm) seam allowance all around the design.

2 Fold the seam allowance to the back of the canvas. Miter the corners and work herringbone stitches to attach it to the back of the canvas. Be sure the stitches do not show on the right side.

3 If a decorative braid or piping is used, pin it to the turned edge of the needlecase and baste in place.

4 Cut the backing fabric ½in (12mm) larger than the finished work.

5 Pin the fabric and canvas with wrong sides together, folding in the hems.

6 Cut narrow ribbon in half and tuck it into the center edges between backing fabric and canvas. Then stitch in place.

7 Slipstitch the backing fabric to the needlecase.

8 If braid or piping is being used, slipstitch to the outside edge, finishing ends.

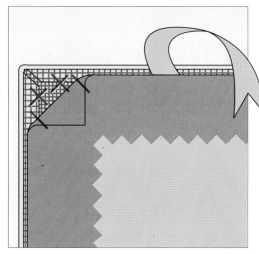

Needlecase, showing narrow ribbon placed between backing fabric and canvas.

9 Use the pinking shears to cut the felt into four or six pieces, each ½in (12mm) smaller than the finished needlecase. Stab stitch to the center of the needlecase to hold in place.

10 Fold needlecase in half. Secure ties. If desired, stitch decorative braid or piping to center of needlecase at fold.

CURTAIN TIEBACKS

▪ Buckram the same size as the finished stretched design or template
▪ Curtain interlining (or domette) the same size as finished design/template
▪ Lining fabric 4in (10cm) larger than the finished design
▪ Plain or decorative cord to fit the finished edges of the tiebacks plus 4in (10cm) extra
▪ Two rings per tieback
▪ Pins

1 Cut the buckram the same size as the template or finished design area.

2 Iron the interlining onto the buckram, using a damp cloth. Trim the interlining to the edge of the buckram.

3 Machine stitch two rows ½in (12mm) from the edge of the worked area of canvas to prevent fraying. Trim to leave a 1in (2.5cm) seam allowance all around the design.

4 Place the buckram on the wrong side of the canvas, with the interlining between the two. Line it up with the finished edge of the design. Baste in place.

5 Clip into the canvas border, taking great care not to cut into the worked area. Dampen the edges of the buckram, then fold the clipped edges of the canvas over onto the damp edges of the buckram and iron down.

6 If decorative cord or other trimmings are used, slipstitch to edge of tiebacks.

7 Cut out a lining ½in (12mm) larger than the finished work. Pin to the tieback, fold under seam allowance and then baste. Finish where necessary and slipstitch around edge.

8 Sew a ring onto the lining at the center point of each of the tieback ends so that they are hidden from the right side.

FLAT SEAT COVER

MATERIALS

■ ⅛ or ¼in (2.5 or 5mm) thick foam the same size as the template or the finished blocked design

■ Synthetic batting large enough to cover both sides of the foam

■ Four lengths of ties or cord to tie cushion to the chair

■ Backing fabric 4in (10cm) larger than the finished design

■ Plain or decorative cord to fit around the finished edge of the design

■ Pins

1 Cut foam the same size as the template or worked design. Trim edges of foam so that they are neat and rounded.

2 Cut the batting into two pieces the same size as the foam. Sandwich the foam between the two pieces of batting and catch-stitch together to hold in place.

3 Machine stitch two or three rows ½in (12mm) from the edge of the worked area to prevent fraying. Trim to leave a 1in (2.5cm) seam allowance around the design.

4 Cut the backing fabric the same size as the trimmed canvas.

5 With the right sides of the fabric and canvas facing, pin or baste together, inserting the ties or cord into the seams at the correct points so they will tie onto the chair. Leave an opening at the back large enough to insert the foam and batting pad. Machine stitch sides together carefully, as close as possible to the worked needlepoint edge. Trim and overcast all raw edges; trim the corners. Turn the cushion right side out.

6 Insert the foam and batting cushion pad. Close opening with slipstitches.

GLASSES CASE

MATERIALS

■ Lining fabric 2in (5cm) larger than the finished, blocked design

■ Decorative cord 2in (5cm) longer than the measurement around the outside edge of the case (optional)

1 Machine stitch as close as possible to the design to prevent fraying.

2 Trim to leave a ⅞in (2cm) seam allowance all around the design.

3 Fold the seam allowance to the back of the canvas and carefully slipstitch to the back of worked stitches.

4 With the wrong sides of the canvas together, fold canvas in half. Herringbone-stitch or overcast together, leaving an opening at the top. Make sure all unworked canvas threads are turned in.

5 Make a lining slightly smaller than the canvas case.

6 With right sides together, sew up bottom and side seams of lining.

7 Slipstitch lining to top opening of canvas to case. Tuck into case.

8 Finish by slipstitching decorative cord around the outside edge.

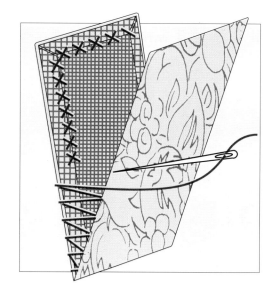

Stitching the sides of the glasses case.

FOOTSTOOL

MATERIALS

■ Round footstool

■ ⅜in (1cm) tacks

■ Strong thread

1 Machine stitch two rows around the blocked design ¾in (2cm) from the edge of the worked area of canvas to prevent fraying. Trim to leave a 1½in (4cm) seam allowance.

2 Using a length of strong cotton threaded in a tapestry needle, sew a row of small running stitches around the circle of the design just inside the machine stitching. Leave enough thread at the beginning and end to act as drawstrings.

3 Place the canvas face down on a flat surface and center the upholstered pad of the footstool onto the center of the canvas.

4 Pull both ends of the drawstrings gently, easing the canvas around the edge of the pad as the thread is pulled tighter. Secure with a bow.

5 Ease the gathers on the back of the footstool pad so there is an even finish round the edge.

6 Tack the canvas onto the underside of the pad ½in (12mm) from the edge, placing the tacks ½ to ¾in (12–20mm) apart from each other.

$\mathscr{S}$TITCH $\mathscr{D}$IRECTORY

The most valuable rule to bear in mind when working stitches is the one which says that as much coverage is required on the back of the canvas as on the front. This ensures that a piece of work which may have taken months or years to complete will be able to withstand more than a lifetime of daily wear and tear.

In the following stitch diagrams, the needle is shown going into and coming out of the canvas in one movement, to show where the next stitch starts. However, I strongly recommend that all stitches are worked with a stabbing movement, with one hand feeding the needle down through the canvas and the other passing it back up.

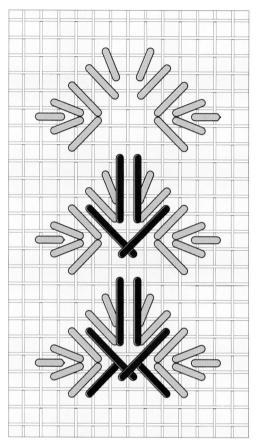

Following the diagram, work in three stages, as follows. Complete all stitches in the first color, add the four large stitches in the second color, then work the last two stitches in the third color.

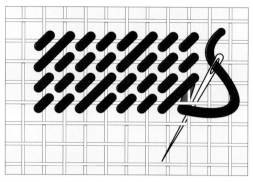

Groups of diagonal stitches are worked over 1,2,1 threads of canvas, filled in between with blocks of four tent stitches.

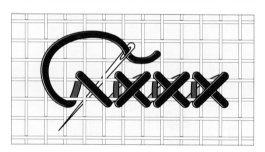

There are many methods of working this stitch and the simplest is to complete each cross before stitching the next. On single mono-thread canvas, work a diagonal stitch over two threads and complete the cross by working a second diagonal stitch in the opposite direction over the top of the first. All crosses must have the top stitch slanting in the same direction so that the stitches lie flat and have a smooth appearance.

On double-thread canvas, use the same method, working each stitch over the intersections of two close threads of canvas.

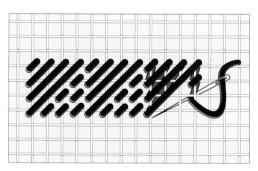

A group of four diagonal stitches worked over 1,2,3,4 intersections of canvas to form a triangle. Six tent stitches are worked to complete the pattern and form a square.

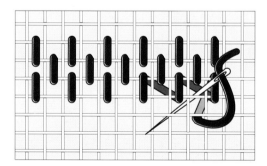

Rows of straight stitches are worked over two threads of canvas with a space of two threads of canvas between each stitch. The next row is started one thread below the first row. The rows interlock.

A group of seven diagonal satin stitches are worked in the same slanting direction to form a square over 1,2,3,4,3,2,1 threads of canvas. A variation can be obtained by alternating the direction of

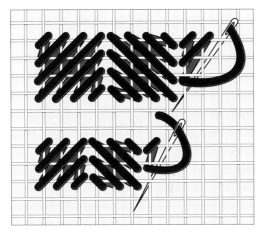

each group of stitches. For a smaller cushion, stitch five diagonal stitches over 1,2,3,2,1 threads of canvas.

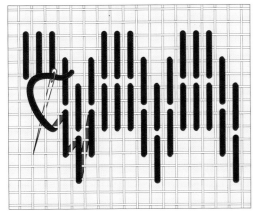

Rows of straight stitches are worked vertically over four threads of canvas, each stitch rising or falling by two threads. The return row interlocks into the first row, repeating the rise and fall of the original stitches.

FLOWER STITCH

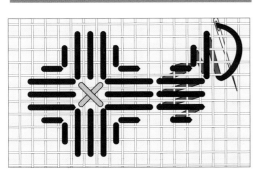

Straight satin stitches worked over 2,4,4,4,2 threads of canvas and worked around to form a flower. The center is filled with a cross stitch.

GOBELIN STITCH (SLANTING)

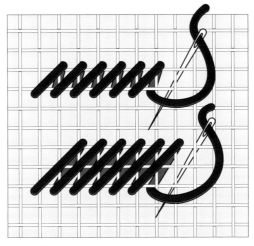

This diagonal stitch can be worked over a varying number of threads and inter-sections, usually no more than ten threads. Take care that the yarn remains untwisted and stitches are worked with an even tension, so that they lie flat and even on the surface of the canvas.

GOBELIN STITCH (STRAIGHT)

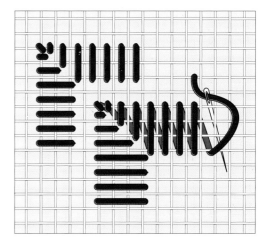

This straight stitch can be worked over any number of threads of canvas. To work a neat mitered corner, follow diagram below.

If a raised texture is needed, lay a strand of yarn along the canvas and work the straight gobelin stitches over the strand. It is important to work this stitch with an even tension and to keep the yarn untwisted so that the stitches lie flat and even on the canvas.

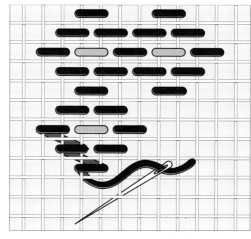

HUNGARIAN VARIATION STITCH I

Eight straight stitches worked over two threads of canvas form a diamond. The center of each pattern is filled in with a straight stitch in a contrasting color. Each diamond is linked to the next.

HUNGARIAN VARIATION II

Eight stitches are worked over one thread of canvas to form a diamond. The center of each pattern is filled with straight stitches over 1,3,1 threads of canvas in a contrasting color. Each diamond is linked to the next.

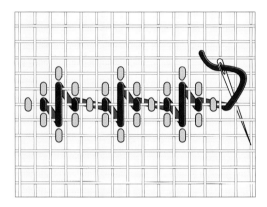

LEAF STITCH

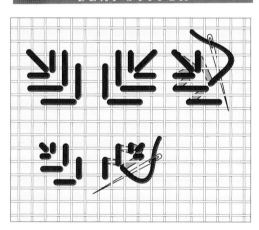

Large Seven straight or diagonal stitches are worked over three and two threads or intersections of canvas. Start with a straight stitch over three threads of canvas and work the other six stitches around to the tip of the leaf and back down to the base.

Small Seven straight or diagonal stitches are worked over one or two threads or intersections of canvas. Start with a straight stitch over two threads of canvas and then work the other six stitches up to the tip of the leaf and back down to the base.

SCOTTISH VARIATION STITCH

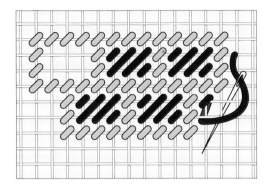

Work the outline of fourteen tent stitches first to form a framework and then fill in with slanting gobelin stitch over 1,2,2,1 intersections of canvas.

TENT STITCH
MONO CANVAS

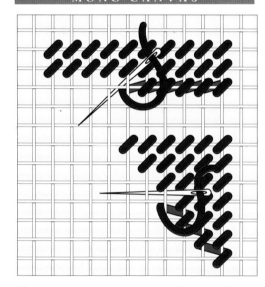

There are two ways to work this stitch: continental and basketweave (both shown on mono and double canvas). All stitches must slant in the same direction.

Continental Work tent stitch in rows horizontally or vertically, using a slanting back stitch so that there is a long stitch on the back of the canvas. When working along a row to the left, stitches will be worked from below the thread to above the thread; on the return row, working to the right, stitches will be worked from above thread to below it.

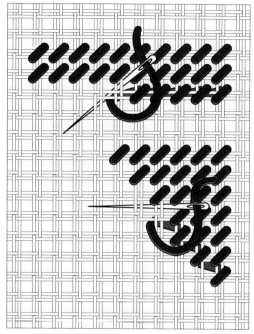

Basketweave Work tent stitch diagonally from the top corner. On down rows, the needle is taken straight down under two horizontal threads of canvas. On up rows, the needle is taken behind two vertical threads of canvas. Be sure to work up rows and down rows alternately.

BEADING

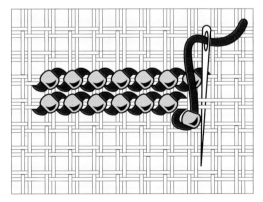

Using a double thickness of thread (not yarn), apply each bead onto the canvas separately. Pick up the bead with the needle and work a diagonal stitch over two close threads of canvas. The beads will lie in the opposite direction to the tent stitch background, which is worked with three strands of crewel yarn.

APPLETON TO PATERNAYAN COLOR CONVERSION CHART

In some cases, there is no exact equivalent shade. An attempt has been made to match the colors as closely as possible, but the finished piece may vary from the finished project shown in the book.

APPLETON	PATERNAYAN	APPLETON	PATERNAYAN	APPLETON	PATERNAYAN
101	313	463	543	745	560
102	313	464	542	746	560
103	312	465	540	747	500
104	312	472	703	751	946
106	310	474	725	752	945
145	911	475	723	753	945
153	514	478	721	754	913
155	533	502	841	755	932
181	475	504	950	756	932
182	463	522	523	757	902
202	406	542	653	758	901
205	872	543	693	759	900
206	871	544	692	822	542
221	490	545	691	823	541
222	933	546	691	825	540
223	923	551	773	831	662
224	931	552	713	832	662
226	930	561	505	833	661
244	641	581	470	835	660
251	653	585	421	841	704
253	693	586	421	842	734
254	692	588	420	843	733
255	651	601	325	844	714
256	650	603	323	861	855
305	400	604	312	863	862
311	751	621	835	871	716
312	752	622	834	872	715
313	751	626	830	873	615
321	513	645	662	874	624
322	513	647	660	875	236
323	512	691	444	877	948
324	512	694	733	881	262
326	511	695	732	884	314
331	644	696	740	911	453
335	n.a.	698	412	925	210
351	605	711	914	941	934
352	605	713	912	943	932
353	604	716	910	945	904
354	603	726	860	963	202
355	603	741	564	976	461
402	612	742	562	991	261
461	564	743	561	992	263
462	544	744	562	996	673

SUPPLIERS

Access Discount Commodities,
PO Box 156, Simpsonville, Maryland 21150

Susan Bates Inc., 212 Middlesex Avenue, Chester, Connecticut 06412
(Tel 203 526 5381)

Gay Bowles Sales Inc., 1310 Plain Field Avenue, PO Box 1060, Janesville, Wisconsin 53547 (Tel 608 754 9466)

Chaparral, 3701 West Alabama, Suite 370, Houston, Texas 77027

Elaine Clabeaux Creative Furnishing (furnire for upholstering), 12357 Sara Glen Drive, Saratoga, California 95070

Dan's Fifth Avenue, 1520 Fifth Avenue, Canyon, Texas 79015

The Elegant Needle Ltd.,
7945 MacArthur Boulevard, Suite 203, Cabin John, Maryland 20818

Ewe Two Ltd., 24 North Merion Avenue, Bryn Mawr, Pennsylvania 19010

Handcraft From Europe, PO Box 31524, San Francisco, California 94131-0524

The Jolly Needlewoman, 5810 Kennett Pike, Centreville, Delaware 19807

Louise's Needlework, 45 N. High Street, Dublin, Ohio 43017

Natalie, 144 N. Larohmont Boulevard, Los Angeles, California 90004

Needlepoint Inc., 251 Post Street, 2nd Floor, San Francisco, California 94108

Needle Works Ltd., 4041 Tulane Avenue, New Orleans, Louisiana 70119

Potpourri, PO Box 78, Redondo Beach, California 90277 (Tel 213 374 1267)

Princess & The Pea, 1922 Parminter Street, Middleton, Wisconsin 53562

Sign Of The Arrow – 1867 Foundation Inc., 9740 Clayton Road, St Louis, Missouri 63124

Village Needlecraft Inc., 7500 S Memorial Pkwy, Unit 116, Huntsville, Alabama 35802

Wilmington Needlework Inc.,
(Stitchery Kits), PO Box 497, Smyna, Delaware 1997
(Tel 302 653-3720)

CANADA

Coats Bell, Canada, 1001 Roselawn Avenue, Toronto, Ontario M6B 1B8
(Tel 416 782 4481)

Dick & Jane, 2352 West 41st Avenue, Vancouver, BC V6M2A4
(Tel 604 266 1090)

The Nimble Thimble, 3201A Yonge Street, Toronto, Ontario M4N 2K9
(Tel 416 483 5462)

Fancyworks, 104–3960 Quera Street, Victoria, BC V8X 4A3

Jet Handcraft Studio Ltd., 1847 Marine Drive, West Vancouver, BC V7V 1J7

S.R. Kertzer Ltd., 105a Winges Road, Woodbridge, Ont L4L 6C2

One Stitch At A Time, Box 114, Picton, Ontario K0K 2T0

The Silver Thimble Inc., 64 Rebecca St, Oakville, Ontario L6J 1J2

NUMBER OF APPLETON THREADS IN THE NEEDLE

CANVAS	TENT STITCH	CROSS STITCH	STRAIGHT STITCH
18#/inch 7#/cm	2 crewel		3 crewel or 1 tapestry
14#/inch 5.5#/cm	2 crewel or 3 crewel or 1 tapestry		4 crewel
12#/inch 5#/cm	3 crewel or 1 tapestry		5 crewel or 6 crewel
8#/inch★ 3#/cm	6 crewel or 2 tapestry	4 crewel or 1 tapestry	8 crewel or 3 tapestry
6#/inch★ 2.5#/cm		8 crewel or 2 tapestry	

★Tent stitch and straight stitch, although quite possible on these coarser canvases, both require a lot of threads in the needle.

NUMBER OF PATERNAYAN THREADS IN THE NEEDLE

CANVAS	TENT STITCH	CROSS STITCH	STRAIGHT STITCH
18#/inch 7#/cm	1 strand		2 strands
14#/inch 5.5#/cm	2 strands		3 strands
12#/inch 5#/cm	2 strands		3 strands
8#/inch★ 3#/cm	1 thread (3 strands)	2 strands	
6#/inch★ 2.5#/cm	4 strands	1 thread (3 strands)	

To work tent stitch using Paternayan Persian yarn, you must divide each thread into three strands. A single strand of Paternayan is slightly thicker than one thread of Appleton Crewel Wool.

$\mathscr{A}$CKNOWLEDGEMENTS

More than anyone else I have to thank my team of stitchers whose beautiful work and kind and gentle comments as they stitched my designs have made this book possible. They are Jane Brierley, Hilary Coe, Katie Dyson, Joan Fuller, Sybil Goodfellow, Rita Hughes, Pat Scottow, and Anne Watson.

For their never-ending support I thank Jane Formby and Jennifer Carr Jones who have lent me their work, my family and friends (especially Janet Haigh) who have encouraged me, given me inspiration and loaned me pieces from their needlework collections.

Thanks also to the Haines family, Angela, David and Nic, who are talented perfectionists and have so beautifully finished many of the needlework projects in this book, and to Elind Frames Ltd., who framed all of the samplers.

I thank Peter Armatage, known to us as "Peter Wools," of Appleton Bros., and his staff, who have supported Stitchery for the last twelve years; their dedication and loyalty to their customers could never be equalled. Thanks to my team at Stitchery, Pat Rattue and Jean and Frank Porter, who have managed to keep things in order even better without my constant interference. Thanks to Vivienne Wells of David & Charles for her quiet and persistent persuasion over the last three years. I hope I have been able to justify her faith in me.

My gratitude to all those who have worked on the design side of this book, supervised by Brenda Morrison at David & Charles – Peter Bridgewater, Tim and Zoe Hill, Angela Kirk, Ethan Danielson, and Susan Rentoul.

Finally I thank Lis Barrett who made it all possible. She coaxed me to the very end, interpreted my manuscript but never changed the meaning, and was always enthusiastic at the right moment.

INDEX

Page references in *italics* indicate illustrations